# Beyond Hummus

*Culinary Treasures of Southern Levant*

# Beyond Hummus

*Culinary Treasures of Southern Levant*

# Basel Nashat Asmar

2050 consulting

First published in the United Kingdom in 2025 by
2050 Consulting
48 Imperial Hall
104-122 City Road
London EC1V 2NR
United Kingdom

Copyright ©Basel Nashat Asmar, 2025

Basel Nashat Asmar has asserted his right under the Copyright, Designs and Patents Act 1988 to be identified as the author of this work.

All rights reserved. No part of this publication may be reproduced, stored in a retrieval system, or transmitted, in any form or by any means, electronic, mechanical, photocopying, recording, or otherwise, without the prior written permission of the publisher.

A CIP for this book is available from the British Library.

ISBN 978-1-917915-00-7

**Author's Notes**:
1. The material in the book made no use of any proprietary data owned by S&P Global, and does not express S&P Global's opinion. The opinions expressed in this book are the responsibility of the author.

2. The use of particular designations of countries or territories does not imply any judgement by the author as to the legal status of such countries or territories, of their authorities and institutions or of the delimitation of their boundaries.

Printed in the United Kingdom

*Cover design by Eman Faidi*

*This book is lovingly written in memory of my uncle, Adnan Doleh, whose appreciation for traditional foods was unmatched, and my aunt, Faizeh Doleh, whose hands brought these dishes to life with love and care.*

# List of Contents

| | |
|---|---:|
| **LIST OF CONTENTS** | vii |
| **ACKNOWLEDGMENTS** | ix |
| **ABOUT THE AUTHOR** | x |
| **INTRODUCTION** | 1 |
| **PART I: POPULAR INGREDIENTS** | 7 |
| Zaatar / Oregano & Thyme | 11 |
|    Zaatar as condiment | 12 |
|    Duqqa | 15 |
|    Zaatar as fresh ingredient | 16 |
| Molokhia / Jute Mallow | 18 |
| Waraq Inab / Vine Leaves | 21 |
|    Husrum / Sour Grapes | 23 |
| Akkoub / Gundelia | 23 |
| Khubeiza / Mallow or Malva | 26 |
| Baqleh / Purslane | 29 |
| Hindba'a / Endive | 31 |
| Louz Akhdar / Fresh Almond | 34 |
| Lift / Turnip | 36 |
|    Turnip leaves and stems | 38 |
| Fakkous / Armenian Cucumber | 39 |
| Freekeh / Roasted Cracked Green Wheat | 41 |
| Summaq / Sumac | 44 |
| Jameed | 47 |
|    Shankleesh | 50 |
|    Kishk | 52 |
| Labaneh / Strained Yogurt | 55 |
| Nabulsi Cheese | 57 |
| **PART II: DISAPPEARING INGREDIENTS** | 61 |
| Kama'a / Desert Truffle | 64 |

| | |
|---|---:|
| Hummedha / Sorrel or Dock | 66 |
| Hamasees / Rumex Pictus | 69 |
| Lsaineh / Jerusalem Salvia | 70 |
| Waraq Toot / Mulberry Leaves | 72 |
| Zamatout / Cyclamen Leaves | 74 |
| Lakhneh / Cauliflower Leaves | 76 |
| Loof / Black Calla | 78 |
| Irqeita / Eminium | 82 |
| Ja'deh / Germander | 84 |
| Hweerneh / Hedge Mustard | 85 |
| Khardal / Mustard Leaves | 87 |
| 'Owainah / Silene | 89 |
| Dhabh / Salsify | 91 |
| Kalakh / Giant Fennel | 93 |
| Kharfeesh / Milk Thistle | 96 |
| Sunnariyah / Golden Thistle | 98 |
| Qurs 'Anna / Eryngo | 99 |
| Murrar / Knapweed | 100 |
| Qataf / Saltbush | 102 |
| Qizha / Nigella Seeds Paste | 104 |
| 'Ijer / Young Watermelon | 105 |
| Habb Qraish / Aleppo Pine Seeds | 107 |
| Ballout / Acorn | 109 |
| Butum / Terebinth | 110 |
| Sidr / Christ's Thorn Jujube | 112 |

## **PART III: DEFINITIONS**  **115**

# Acknowledgments

I would like to thank my beloved mother Fairouz Taha Doleh,[1] who contributed heavily to this manuscript, translating, suggesting and adding valuable information, and editing the Arabic version of this book. I am also thankful to my brothers, sisters-in-law, and nephews, Sanad and Qais, the picky foodies, as well as my friends in the UK, Jordan, the USA, and the UAE, for their encouragement and support throughout this interesting writing process. Special thanks to Samer Hattar for his invaluable notes.

Once again, completion of this book would not have been possible without the efforts of Karen Hall, who not only edited my manuscript meticulously, but also raised sharp questions and shared valuable insights which influenced the final book shape.

---

[1] Fairouz Taha Doleh has had a distinguished career in education spanning over 40 years, serving in various roles such as teacher, headteacher, and consultant. Her dedication to the field of education has significantly impacted the lives of many students and educators. Fairouz holds a BA in History and advanced education certificates, which have provided her with a strong foundation and expertise in her field.
After retiring, she continues to lead an active and fulfilling life. She is an avid reader and enjoys spending her time immersed in books, gardening, and cherishing moments with her grandchildren. She also contributes to her community by serving as a board member of several charities, demonstrating her commitment to giving back and helping others. She lives in Amman, Jordan, where she continues to inspire those around her with her wisdom and compassion.

# About the Author

***Basel Nashat Asmar*** is an expert in oil and gas fundamentals, costs, and technology, as well as a dynamic simulation expert with extensive computer, modelling, and simulation skills. He is currently a Director with S&P Global, based in London, UK. Dr. Asmar has previously held roles with major engineering companies involved in large liquefied natural gas (LNG) regasification and liquefaction terminals, natural gas compression stations, and offshore oil and gas production platforms. As a senior process engineer and dynamic simulation specialist, he has worked with CB&I (currently McDermott), Mott MacDonald, and IMEG, and as a lead consultant with 2050 Consulting Ltd and Trident Consultants Ltd. His academic background includes a position as a research associate at the University of Nottingham.

*Basel Asmar*

Besides his extensive professional experience, Dr. Asmar is also an accomplished author with four books to his name and over 50 articles published in international journals, conference proceedings, newspapers, and electronic media. He has also authored more than 60 technical reports. Dr. Asmar is a Chartered Engineer, a member of the Institution of Chemical Engineers (IChemE), a senior member of the American Institute of Chemical Engineers (AIChE), and a member of the Jordanian Engineers Association.

Despite his deep expertise in engineering and technology, Dr. Asmar also has a passion for writing on diverse subjects such as politics, history, and food, showcasing his versatility and broad intellectual interests. He holds a BSc in Chemical Engineering from the University of Jordan, an MSc in Process and Project Engineering, and a PhD in Chemical Engineering from the University of Nottingham, as well as a doctorate in Geoscience from Freie Universität Berlin, Germany.

# Introduction

The cookbook industry is thriving despite the explosion of digital media, where one can watch millions of hours of cooking recipes or explore apps for thousands of variations for each recipe that mutate fast.

Thus, in deciding to write this book, I made the conscious choice not to write a traditional recipe book, but rather a brief guide exploring ingredients which are either unknown in the West or becoming almost unheard of in the Southern Levant (Jordan and Palestine), with some of them can be classified analogously as 'extinct'.

When one mentions Levantine or Eastern Mediterranean cuisine, most think of the internationally popular Lebanese cuisine.

Besides the three pillars of Mediterranean cuisine: olive for oil, wheat for bread and grape for wine, most will be thinking of the ubiquitous Levantine ingredients like chickpea, tahini, aubergine/eggplant, olives, pomegranate, bulgur, lamb, yogurt and exotic spices. With notable scarcity of seafood, compared to many other cuisines.

There are several Levantine dishes that have become well-known in the Western world. Amongst the most famous are falafel, kebabs, kibbeh, tabouleh and baba ganouj.

However, besides these famous dishes and the ingredients that broke through, there are a multitude of other flavours, textures and combinations that are there to be discovered. Indeed, many of the most popular ones have not yet crossed over into internationally celebrated widely consumed categories, but remain relatively unknown, waiting to get their chances.

Nevertheless, with the globalisation of the food supply chain, many of the local, traditionally used ingredients are falling out of favour in many parts of the world as younger generations are moving to adopt a more homogenised selection of universal and fusion dishes.

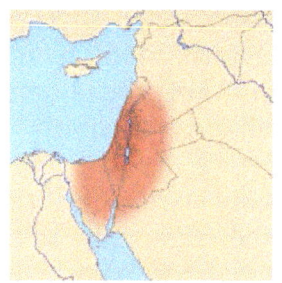

In this book I attempt to explore some of those popular ingredients from the **Southern Levant** area, covering Jordan, historic Palestine, the adjacent border areas in Southern Lebanon, Southern Syria and North Sinai.

This Southern Levant region shares a lot of its cuisine with the Northern Levant, indeed with the overall Levantine cuisine, which goes back thousands of years, is known to many

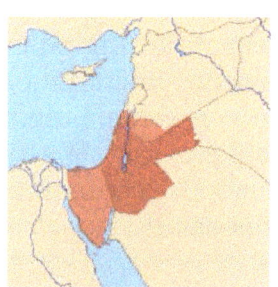

*Southern Levant*

Westerners as 'Lebanese'. While it is steeped in tradition, it was also influenced by many cuisines such as those of the Persian, Byzantine and Ottoman Empires, who all ruled the region at different points, influencing its gastronomic habits. Moreover, being at the edge of the dessert, the cuisine in the Southern Levant shares some ingredients, methods of cooking and recipes with the Arabian Peninsula. Furthermore, due to centuries of population mixing, it also shares many traditions with Egypt.

Recently as a result of the numerous migrations into the region, different methods and other traditions from the wider Arab world, have been absorbed into modern cuisine. The popularity and prevalence of cooking programs, on all platforms, have also introduced many other regional recipes, as well as those from further afield, so we are seeing the evolution of a unique combining of these international influences.

In the UK alone, over 50% of British chefs and 'foodies' have stated that they like to experiment with new cooking trends and ingredients. This percentage increases with younger people.[2]

---

[2] https://www.mintel.com/press-centre/food-and-drink/60-of-uk-16-34-year-olds-who-cook-like-experimenting-with-new-cooking-trends-but-many-fail-to-master-the-basics

Another interesting trend is the mixing two or more cuisines, creating exciting fusion cooking.

The book is divided into three parts: 'Part I: Popular Ingredients', which covers well known ingredients, often used locally, but not internationally; 'Part II: Disappearing Ingredients', which covers food that were once commonly consumed but are less popular nowadays, whose ingredients are hardly known, or rarely used, even in the Levant; and finally, 'Part III: Definitions' which defines certain terms and names of recipes often served in the Southern Levant.

In this book, I concentrate on several Levantine ingredients not common in the West (or hardly known), but that are popularly used in the Levant. Thus, I do not dwell on chickpea or hummus as such ingredient, it is widely available all over the West.

It is worth saying that the preparation of many traditional dishes was time consuming, laborious and complicated. With the development of new kitchen equipment and the production of ready-prepared ingredients – many of these dishes are much simpler and quicker to prepare. While traditionalists and purists advocate using only traditional grandmothers' methods to label the dishes 'authentic', in reality better, less time-consuming results can be obtained if some of the difficult steps are bypassed, and ready half-prepared ingredients are used.

If one goes shopping in the UK or US in an ordinary local supermarket, many of the ingredients described in this book will not be found. Occasionally perhaps some of them can be found as finished products or packaged readymade foods (e.g. vine leaves). So, this book is meant as a guide to *the ingredients* that are used in many recipes or dishes, and not a cookery book. I stress on this point. Once you learn more about these ingredients, then you will be able to find them, follow interesting recipes and experiment with them at your leisure.

With widely available access to the internet, with vast libraries of information on every conceivable topic imaginable, for those who cook, apps like Cookpad and YouTube have provided millions of recipes, from professionals and keen amateurs, at the touch of a button/icon. Despite this, the number of cookery books being published continues to increase. I reiterate, this is not another cookery book. I aim to open a window on particular ingredients, inviting people to try them. Using apps such as Cookpad or YouTube they can find an abundance of recipes.

In many cases when recipes involve unfamiliar ingredients, most people will not want the inconvenience of having to get the ingredients. Here I attempted to give some guidance on availability, where one can source such ingredients in the US and the UK, as well as in the Southern Levant. I have also highlighted which ingredients are becoming more familiar products and can be found at mainstream supermarkets or big ethnic shops.

[Note - what is sometimes referred to as one distinct ingredient can, in reality, be two related plants or species, but people mistakenly think of them as one ingredient or two variations of the same plant. This is an important distinction as it can lead to a very different flavour in the dish you are preparing.]

# Part I

# Popular Ingredients

In Part 1 I discuss several ingredients that range from the ubiquitous to quite common in the Southern Levant, despite being hardly known by most people in the UK or the USA. It is important to clarify that when I say 'hardly known', I am referring to the current way that the ingredient is used as a food or in a dish, e.g. almonds are very well known as a nut, whereas eating green almond fruit is not known.

The ingredients I explore include vegetables, fruits, grains/cereals, spices and dairy products. Note that the label 'fruit' or 'vegetable' may refer to the cultural use of the ingredient rather than its botanical definition, e.g. people often refer to tomatoes as vegetables, when actually, they are fruits. In order to avoid confusion, here I use the most common opinion or public perception.

Although most of the ingredients covered in Part 1 are uncommon to many people in the UK or the US, more recently, they can be found relatively easily in these countries, either in supermarkets or ethnic shops. It goes without saying that they can be found everywhere in the Southern Levant.

In the developed world, technology has meant that cooking methods have moved on from the old traditional ways of gathering, washing, peeling, grinding or cooking ingredients, to using food processors, microwaves, air friers, etc. All this equipment can be utilised to enhance recipes and make the cooking process much more efficient, etc. In my opinion, these methods are still considered part of the cooking process, and I disagree with those purists who only acknowledge 'authentic cooking', i.e. if it was done from first step of gathering and preparing the raw ingredients. In fact, for me, there is no benefit in creating things from scratch if we can save time, money or both by using modern methods and equipment.

For those with the opportunity and means to use modern methods, this attitude now is widespread and broadly accepted. Almost no-one in the Southern Levant will cook baklava at home, instead, buying it from the sweet shop is usual. The same attitude is accepted with many of the most popular dishes, like hummus and falafel.

The ingredients covered here are essential to gastronomic life in the Southern Levant, even though most in the West are not aware of them. These ingredients though, only tell part of the story, as many other popular ingredients are equally, if not more, important in the Southern Levant but are also now eaten extensively in the West. The most popular ones are hummus (chickpea/garbanzo bean), lentils, aubergine (eggplant) and tahini (sesame paste). Okra (lady's fingers) is essential in the Southern Levant, but while its use is limited in the UK and most of the US, it is popular in Southern US, hence I have not included it in this book.

# Zaatar / Oregano & Thyme

Also spelled za'atar or zatar (Arabic: زعتر). This is an indispensable ingredient in any household in the Southern Levant. Zaatar is the undisputed king of Palestinian and Jordanian herbs. The usage of the name is complicated as the word can refer to several types of a family of related Middle Eastern culinary herbs. There are different dialects of the Levant, thus oregano, thyme and marjoram can sometimes be referred to as zaatar or mardakosh. While in most dictionaries the word 'thyme' is translated as zaatar in Arabic, people in the Southern Levant associate the world mostly with 'oregano'. In fact, these herbs are loosely related Mediterranean plants, so it is unsurprising that they could be used interchangeably.

For culinary purposes, in this book, we refer to zaatar as the fresh herb that can be used in many recipes as a main

*Zaatar*

*thyme*

*oregano*

ingredient, the dried herb alone[3] or as a mixture or blend of spices, which is used as a condiment in many recipes as well.

Zaatar is a staple food in the Levant. It is well-known in the entire Middle East and North Africa.

## *Zaatar as condiment*

As a prepared condiment, zaatar has many variations that differ from region to region or between families. Recipes are often kept secret. In general, the mixture is made with several main ingredients:

1. Ground or crushed dried oregano[4], thyme, marjoram, summer savory, or some combination of these herbs
2. Toasted sesame seeds.
3. Salt.
4. Other spices such as sumac, cumin, caraway, coriander, anise seed or fennel seed.
5. Other ingredients including ground roasted chickpea, pistachio, peanut; or citric acid powder (sour salt).

---

[3] Dried zaatar can be thyme, oregano, marjoram or summer savory depending on the nomenclature used in a specific geographic area in Southern Levant

[4] One of the oregano varieties is what is referred to as Bible or Biblical hyssop.

Some commercial and cheaper varieties also include roasted flour as a filler.

The condiment zaatar is prepared by blending crushed dried oregano, thyme, marjoram, sumac, toasted sesame seeds and salt, or whatever combination of ingredients is used. It is sometimes then rubbed with olive oil to darken its colour and smoothen its texture. However, as with any ancient or traditional spice blend, there are many variations with plenty of opinions about which is the right proportion for each ingredient and which ingredients should be included.

The texture of the mix is not of a powdered fine spice blend, but rather free flowing coarse herbs with a nutty flavour from the toasted sesame seeds.[5]

Numerous blends can be bought loose from deli-like counters in Southern Levant supermarkets, speciality shops, spice merchants or readily pre-packaged, off the shelves.

*packaged zaatar*

In the US and the UK, pre-packaged blends can be bought from some mainstream supermarkets, farmers or street markets and from many ethnic shops, where some offer specialised counters. It is also available at many online stores worldwide, or via delivery apps.

---

[5] https://www.eatzaatar.com/pages/what-is-zaatar

The most famous blends are:

1. Palestinian (colour: green), with oregano and sumac as main ingredients.
2. Lebanese (colour: reddish), with oregano and more sumac as the main ingredients. Hence the reddish colour.
3. Aleppo (colour: brownish), with oregano, sumac roasted ground chickpea and peanut as the main ingredients. Hence the brownish colour.

One important character of zaatar is that it is not perishable.

Zaatar can be found or eaten as:

1. A dip – eaten alone, or in sandwiches with olive oil (a favourite school kids' sandwich). It is often sold as the main filling for ka'ak al-Quds – although as kids we were always warned that this variety of zaatar was cheap, containing a lot of unhealthy sour salt instead of better-quality ingredients or components.
2. Manaqeesh - the main topping ingredient.
3. Mix or sprinkled on top in certain dairy products, e.g.

*Zaatar dip*

*ka'ak al-Quds*

*manaqeesh*

labaneh and shankleesh.
4. Added as a condiment or seasoning to salads.
5. Used in mawaleh.
6. Breadsticks rolled in zaatar.

## *Duqqa*

Also spelled as dukka (Arabic: دقة). This is also a condiment made with a blend of spices. Technically, duqqa is not zaatar, as it does not contain the main ground green ingredient, but it often contains the other ingredients and has the same texture. The colour of duqqa is always brownish, with different shades, depending on the components. Due to these similarities, it is often associated with zaatar, especially as a dip.

Similar to zaatar, duqqa has many blend variations. The most famous regional varieties are:

*duqqa*

1. Palestinian - composed on ground roasted wheat, lentils, chickpeas, cumin, coriander seeds, caraway seeds, dill, roasted sesame seeds, sumac, salt, sour salt and powdered chilli.
2. Egyptian - composed of ground roasted chickpeas, peanuts, cumin, caraway seeds, salt and roasted sesame seeds.
3. Hijazi - composed of ground

roasted cumin, coriander seeds, black pepper, salt, roasted sesame seeds, sour salt and dried rose petals.
4. Syrian - composed of ground roasted wheat, almonds, cumin, coriander seeds, fennel seeds, black pepper, salt, roasted sesame seeds and small amount of oregano.

Duqqa is prepared in similar way as zaatar, is eaten as a dip in an identical way and its ways of being used are also similar.

## *Zaatar as fresh ingredient*

In the Southern Levant, the term 'green zaatar' (Arabic: زعتر أخضر, pronounced za'atar akhdar) refers to the shrub-like plant known as Origanum syriacum, which is known in English as Syrian oregano, Lebanese oregano or Biblical hyssop. In Southern Levant there are two varieties, domesticated and wild, with the latter having sharper taste. The fresh leaves of this plant are used as main ingredients in salads and pastries, as well as a seasoning or flavouring (منكه) in several meat and poultry dishes.

In addition, once dried, it is used as a herb in several meat and poultry dishes.

The fresh leaves can also be used as tea

or added to tea. There are currently several brands of green zaatar teabags that exist, although the terminology can be confusing as many use 'thyme' in English since it is the more widely known name.

In the Southern Levant, the fresh leaves are abundant and are widely available in grocery stores etc in season. They are often also sold by street and roadside vendors when in season in the spring.

In the US or the UK, it is difficult to obtain the fresh leaves at mainstream outlets and it is infrequently stocked in ethnic shops when in season. It is sometimes listed on online outlets.

The vegetable can be preserved domestically either dried or frozen. However, its availability in frozen or canned forms commercially is limited.

Zaatar akhdar has several culinary uses in the Sothern Levant. These include:

1. The leaves are used in salads as main or supplementary ingredient.
2. In several pastries, as a filling or top, including traditional fatayer/aqras, or open ones (like sfeiha) or mutabbaq.
3. With eggs in an omelette, often with white cheese.
4. As a topping on pizza.

*aqras zaatar*

# Molokhia / Jute Mallow

Also spelled as mulukhiyah, moloukhiyya, mloukiya (Arabic: ملوخية) is a leaf vegetable, where the leaves are eaten but the root, stem, flowers and fruits are not.[6] It has several names in English including jute mallow, Jew's mallow, corchorus, nalta jute and tossa jute.

*molokhia leaves*

With some theories suggesting its name in Arabic is derived from 'royal', this is considered the queen of vegetables in many Middle Eastern households.

*molokhia plant*

In the Southern Levant, molokhia is often bought from grocery stores, supermarkets, or even from the back of trucks or by roadside in its fresh form, either as full stems/bunches or the plucked leaves alone (mwarraqa). Recently it can be bought already chopped from many stores.

In the US and the UK, the vegetable is still uncommon but is available, mostly frozen or dried, in ethnic shops and supermarkets. It may be labelled with the Arabic name, jute leaves or its African names (e.g. ewedu, muera), Filipino name (saluyot) or Haitian name (lalo). Although it can sometimes be found canned in brine (see Amazon)

*frozen molokhia*

*dried molokhia*

---

[6] The flowers and pods are eaten in other cuisines.

or even, but seldom, found fresh.

Molokhia can be stored frozen or dried. The latter form of storage is in decline as the frozen variety (whole leaves or chopped) is more popular.

Molokhia is one of the most loved foods in the Middle East. Parents introduce their kids to the dish at very young age and I can say with confidence that the majority love it. The leaves have been cooked in the region for thousands of years and the way molokhia has been cooked hardly changed. This is one of the recipes that does not include ingredients from the 'New World'.

While many variations exist, there are two main recipes that dominate the Southern Levant. The difference is in the way that the vegetable is used. These are:

1. Molokhia Na'emah, (i.e. fine chopped), which uses the chopped leaves. The dish is basically a soup based on meat or poultry broth. A vegetarian version can be cooked and is popular when fasting in Lent. It is served with white rice, vermecelli rice or flat bread, accompanied with lemon juice, fried bread, vinegar and chopped onion sauce. Chopped leaves method is the form used in Egypt (where it is the national dish),

*molokhia na'imah*

Sudan and the Arab Peninsula.
2. Molokhia Waraq, (i.e. whole leaves), which uses unchopped leaves cooked as a stew, with or without meat, or poultry and also served with rice or flat bread. It is the preferred method cooked mostly in Northern Levant.

*molokhia waraq*

Other recipes are also used, these include:

1. Bissara, which is a dip-consistency dish made of dried fava beans and molokhia, often eaten with flat bread, with lots of lemon.
2. New creative inventions by chefs such as fritters (substitute spinach or khubeiza) or type of open fatayer (pastries).

*bissara*

The vegetable is also eaten widely in West Africa, East Africa, Haiti, Philippines, parts of the Indian Subcontinent and China, and has become widely used in Japan in the last two decades.

Recently, popular ready prepared molokhia meals have increased their reach and can be bought as:
1. Microwaveable ready meal in Egypt, Jordan and the UK (in the Levantine recipe soup).
2. Ready-to-eat in jars.

*microwaveable molokhia ready meals*

*ready-to-eat molokhia jar*

3. As a baby food product.

*baby food molokhia*

## Waraq Inab / Vine Leaves

Grape is one of the 'trinity' or 'triad' of basic ingredients in Mediterranean cuisine, (the other two being wheat and olives).

*vine leaves*

Grapes are one of the major agricultural crops globally and besides being globally eaten as fruits, they are also fermented to produce vinegar, wine and other alcoholic beverages. In addition, the dried fruits are preserved as raisins which are common in both desserts and savoury dishes.

Here we are only talking about the vine or grape leaves. In most countries where vines are cultivated, the leaves are discarded, but in the Eastern Mediterranean and Southeastern Europe, they are a staple food.

In the Southern Levant, Waraq Inab is often bought from grocery stores or supermarkets, both in fresh or in brine/pickled or dried forms and recently, frozen. It can also be obtained from roadside vendors in its fresh form. Moreover, many families harvest it from their vine trees or get it from

*frozen vine leaves*

neighbours and relatives.

In the US and the UK, the vegetable is available mostly in the brined/pickled or frozen forms in ethnic shops and supermarkets. Although it can sometimes be found in the dried form or occasionally may be found fresh.

Waraq Inab can be preserved as pickled, in brine, canned or frozen. It can be stored dried, but this is declining in popularity.

*vine leaves in brine*

In the Southern Levant there are several ways where vine leaves are used:

1. Stuffed as waraq inab or dawali – with rice, bulgur, or freekeh, chopped parsley, herbs, spices and sometimes minced meat. Often cooked together with stuffed courgette/zucchini.
2. Eaten raw accompanying tabbouleh.

*stuffed vine leaves*

New creative recipes are using it as:

1. A substitute filling in pastry parcels (fatayer) replacing spinach.
2. Making grape vine cake – place rice, herbs, spices, sometimes meat, between two layers made of many leaves, then bake.
3. Use them as a wrapping for stuffed artichokes or broad beans stuffing.

Stuffed vine leaves are available, ready to eat, in cans, frozen or fresh at supermarkets, pre-packaged or at deli counters – although exclusively the vegetarian version.

*ready-to-eat stuffed vine leaves*

## *Husrum / Sour Grapes*

Husrum (Arabic: حصرم) is the unripe grape that can be collected when sour. In the Southern Levant it has unique culinary uses:

1. Pickled
2. A main ingredient in a dish called husrumiyyeh, which is husrum cooked with whole lentils.
3. Dibis husrum and used as substitute to lemon juiceز

*husrum*

*dibis husrum*

# Akkoub / Gundelia

Akkoub (Arabic: عكوب; sometimes pronounced ka'oub كعوب), also spelled akoub. This is a thistle-like, thorny flowering plant, native to the Eastern Mediterranean. It is known in English by the name gundelia[7] or the common name tumbe thistle. The plant is a

*akkoub stems and undeveloped flowerheads*

---

[7] Scientific name is Gundelia tournefortii.

23

popular edible ingredient in the Eastern Mediterranean and Kurdistan. It grows wild and is not yet cultivated. It is a very versatile vegetable and almost all its parts are edible, including the leaves, stems, roots, the undeveloped flowerheads/inflorescence and the seeds.

*akkoub plant*

This vegetable divides opinion. Some view it as a poor cousin of the artichoke, whereas others consider it the star of the thorny vegetables. The akkoub plant needs to be de-thorned thoroughly before being used as a culinary ingredient and this unpleasant process is hated by many. It even has its own unique verb describing it (Arabic: عكب).

In the Southern Levant, Akkoub is available in mainstream grocery shops or supermarkets in season, often pre-cleaned and dethorned (معكب جاهز). They can also be bought fresh (with thorns) in markets and from roadside vendors when in season. Since they grow wild, they can also be collected from the wild.

In the US and the UK, the plant is not readily available commercially at mainstream supermarkets or grocery stores. It can be seldom obtained from speciality ethnic stores or online in the dried form.

To preserve, the de-thorned vegetable, it is blanched then cooled and frozen. Note that this process needs to be done shortly after de-thorning as otherwise the thorns will grow again if left to next day. It can also be stored in brine or dried.

The vegetable is eaten in the Middle East, where it is popular in Palestine, Jordan, Lebanon and amongst the Kurds in Northern Iraq. In the Southern Levant it is eaten in season and is cooked as:

*akkoub in brine*

1. The undeveloped flowerheads, peeled stems and young leaves are sautéed with olive oil and diced onion, served with flat bread.
2. With egg, as mufarrakeh or ijjeh.
3. Stewed with or without yogurt, served with white rice.
4. As maqloubeh.
5. As a kibbeh.
6. As a filling in fatayer.
7. As a filling in karadesh al-mahshouk, which is made of corn flour dough filled with onion, tomatoes and akkoub, then baked.
8. Another dish is to put a trimmed inflorescence in a meatball, fry these in olive oil and then simmer them in a sauce containing lemon juice.

*stewed akkoub with yogurt*

In Israel, collecting the plant from the

wild, to sell it as edible vegetable in the market by the Arab citizens, resulted in a decline in the plant population thereby threatening it. Thus, it is considered a preserved wild plant and collecting it is restricted to personal use. However, since most Arabs see this rule as a discriminatory and provocative act, as a form of resistance, its usage increased in the Palestinian Territories.

# Khubeiza / Mallow or Malva

Khubeizah, Khubeza, Khubeizeh or Khobeiza are amongst various alternative spellings (Arabic: خبازة or خبيزة) for this wild plant, which has been used for millennia as a leafy vegetable. Its leaves, stem, flowers, fruits (seed pods), seeds and roots[8] can all be eaten.

*khubeiza leaves and plant*

Its common name in Arabic translates to 'small loaf or dwarf bread', because its edible seeds are flat and round like Arab bread (pitta).

It has several names in English including mallow, malva, cheeses, buttonweed or cheeseplant.[9] It is the common variety of mallow (some of

---

[8] Mallow roots release a thick mucus when boiled in water. The thick liquid that is created can be beaten to make a meringue-like substitute for egg whites. Boiling peeled seed pods can lead to same result. Note that the sap that was used for marshmallows historically is extracted from the roots of the cousin plant marshmallow plant (Althaea officinalis).
[9] Scientific name is Malva sylvestris, Malva nicaensis, Malva parviflora, and Malva neglecta.

several closely related genera in the Malvaceae family to bear the common English name mallow) that is used as culinary ingredient. It also has medicinal and ornamental uses.

The plant grows wild and is abundantly available when in season. Very limited attempts have been made to commercially cultivate it.

In the Southern Levant, the vegetable is abundant, and it is often collected from the wild. After being neglected for years, khubeiza is increasingly being offered in mainstream outlets, supermarkets and often sold by street or roadside vendors when in season in the spring.

In the US or the UK, it is hard to obtain the vegetable. It is not available in mainstream outlets and is only sometimes stocked in ethnic shops. It is seldom found at farmers markets. It is sometimes listed by online outlets. Certainly, those who are keen can collect it from the wild.

As with other green leafy vegetables, coarsely chopped khubeiza leaves can be stored frozen either after blanching or directly from fresh, by going through a pre-freezing process first.[10] Neither

---

[10] Pre-freezing process is done by spreading the fresh greens on a baking sheet in the freezer for 2-3 hours. The freezing process is then completed by moving the greens to airtight containers or well-sealed freezer bags.

canned nor frozen khubeiza leaves are available commercially.

Khubeiza has several culinary uses in the Sothern Levant. These include:

1. Sautéed (chopped or whole) in olive oil and onion.
2. With eggs, sautéed as mufarrakeh or as an omelette.
3. Using the leaves simmered or boiled as side dish.
4. Steamed with garlic and tomatoes, and eaten as an appetiser.
5. Boiled with balls of dough (bahboutha).
6. The young leaves (and flowers) are used in salads as substitute to spinach, lettuce or cabbage.
7. In soups as a main ingredient, or substitute molokhia (see above).
8. As pilaf with rice (called shakhtoura), bulgur or semolina, or can have a soup-like consistency.
9. Used in stews with or without meat and chickpea as substitute to spinach. It is served with plain rice.
10. Stuffing the leaves with bulgur or rice, with or without meat, similar to waraq inab (see above).
11. In several pastries as a filling or

*sautéed khubeiza*

*stuffed khubeiza leaves*

top including traditional fatayer/aqras or open ones (like sfeiha).
12. In fried patties or fritters made of khubeiza leaves, combined with bulgur, breadcrumbs, eggs, spices, garlic and onions.
13. The small fruit can be eaten raw and is particularly popular among children.

Outside the Levant, the vegetable is also eaten around the Mediterranean (Turkey, Greece, Italy, Egypt and North Africa) but it fell out of favour in other European countries. Khubeiza is eaten in some parts of India. The roots are also used in some Chinese soups. It is also used as a medicine or herbal supplement, in many other countries including Iran and China.

## Baqleh / Purslane

Baqleh/Purslane, which is also spelled as bakleh, ba'leh or bagleh, amongst many variations of spellings (Arabic: بقلة), is a green leaf vegetable that can be eaten raw or cooked. Colloquially it is known as 'little hogweed'.[11] The leaves, stems, flowers and seeds of the baqleh plant, are all edible.

*baqleh leaves and plant*

The plant name 'baqleh', used in

---

[11] Scientific name is Portulaca oleracea.

Southern Levant, is the name commonly used in standard Arabic. However, the vegetable has numerous regional names. These include farfahina (Arabic: فرفحينة) in the Levant, rigleh (Arabic: رجلة) in Egypt, barbin (Arabic: بربين) in Iraq, baqla mubarakah and barbir (Arabic: بقلة مباركة or بربير) in the Gulf, zhanab al-faras (Arabic: ذنب الفرس) in Yemen, bundlaq (Arabic: بندلاق) in Tunisia, bleibsha (Arabic: بليبشة) in Libya, and burtlaq (Arabic: برطلاق) in Algeria.

As with khubeiza, in the Southern Levant, this vegetable grows wild and is abundantly available when in season. Its footprint now extends globally. Very limited attempts have been made to commercially cultivate it. It is available in mainstream outlets - at supermarkets, grocery shops and from roadside vendors when in season. It is also possible to collect it from the wild.

In the US and the UK, it can sometimes be found in ethnic shops and is sometimes listed on online outlets. Certainly, those familiar with the plant and can safely recognise it, can forage for it in the countryside.

The vegetable can be preserved frozen. However, it is not available commercially, frozen or canned, yet.

Baqleh has several culinary uses in the Southern Levant. Generally, it can substitute spinach or khubeiza in many recipes. Methods of culinary uses include:

1. Sautéed (chopped or whole) in olive oil, tomatoes and onion.
2. With eggs, sautéed or as an omelette.
3. Steamed with garlic and tomatoes, and eaten as an appetiser.
4. Used in salads, most notably fattoush or with yogurt.
5. In soups as a main ingredient.
6. Used in stews with or without meat and chickpea or lentil as substitute to spinach. It is served with plain rice.
7. In several pastries as a filling or top including traditional fatayer/aqras or open ones (like sfeiha).

*baqleh stew*

*fatayer baqleh*

Baqleh is eaten everywhere except in the US and, to a lesser extent, the UK, where it fell out of favour. However, it is making a comeback in those two countries, with several celebrity chefs rediscovering its many uses.

# Hindba'a / Endive

Hindba'a (Arabic: هندباء), also spelled Hindbeh (Arabic: هندبة), is a family of leaf vegetables eaten in the Eastern

*endive plant and leaves*

Mediterranean. The name covers several bitter-leafed species that fall under the genus Cichorium. These include the species commonly known as endive,[12] wild endive[13] and common chicory.[14]

*common chicory plant and leaves*

Although botanically it is not the same genus, several species of the genus Taraxacum (Arabic: طرخشقون), commonly known as dandelion are also called hindba'a at many local communities. The label 'dandelion' is commonly used in many cookbooks when this Levantine leafy plant is included in their recipes.

*wild endive plant and leaves*

These similarities in appearance, combined with the numerous variations of their names between different dialects can cause great confusion between the two genera. This can be seen when we consider their local names in Arabic, where this plant alone is known by at least five different names, including 'alt (Arabic: علت), chicoria (Arabic: شيكوريا), tarkhshacon (Arabic: طرخشقون), saris (Arabic: سريس), and asnan al-asad (Arabic: أسنان الأسد). In Lebanon, Taraxacum has other local names, including saliqa (Arabic: سليقة) and mukhu bi-'ibu (Arabic: مخو بعبه). It is important to be aware of this when shopping for the ingredients listed in

*dandelion plant*

*tarkhshacon*

---

[12] Scientific name is Cichorium endivia.
[13] Scientific name is Cichorium pumilum.
[14] Scientific name is Cichorium intybus.

the recipe you are using.

In fact, both leafy plants are similar and, in many Levantine markets, sold interchangeably and used in similar fashions. Both are entirely edible, but in general, the leaves are the section of the plant used for culinary reasons.

In Southern Levant it can be bought fresh from grocery stores and supermarkets, when in season. They are also obtained from street and roadside vendors.

In the US or the UK, this vegetable can be found in some mainstream supermarkets and grocery shops. Note however, that sometimes a different variety (related species) is stocked. It can also be found in ethnic shops, and it is sometimes listed on online outlets.

As with other green leafy vegetables, coarsely chopped hindba'a leaves can be stored at home frozen, either after blanching or directly from fresh, by going through a pre-freezing process first. The frozen leaves are not available commercially. It is also dried and used as tea.

Hindba'a has several culinary uses in the Sothern Levant which include:

1. Boiled then sautéed (chopped) in olive oil, and onion (sometimes with tahini or yogurt).

*hindbeh bi zeit (sauted hindba'a)*

2. Used in fresh salads with a combination of diced onion, lemon juice, olive oil, and tomatoes.
3. In soups as a main ingredient or added to other soups.
4. Stewed with minced meat or chicken.
5. Used as an ingredient in a sauce with pasta and sausages.
6. In several pastries as a filling in traditional fatayer/aqras with onion or white cheese.

# Louz Akhdar / Fresh Almond

In the eyes of most people, the almond is a widely available, edible nut, that can be eaten raw or toasted, used in numerous desserts, in breakfast cereals, as a topping, garnish or embellishment to many sweet or savoury dishes. In fact, this nut is an edible dry seed from the almond fruit, obtained by removing the fleshy outer greenish grey covering and the inner hard shell.

*green almonds*

The almond seed has numerous other usages, in the form of oil or almond milk.

When the fruit is still immature, it is called louz akhdar (literally green almond – Arabic: لوز أخضر). It is a tangy and tender fruit that is popular in the

Southern Levant when in season, (a relatively short period from April to early June).

When in season, fresh louz akhdar is widely available at grocery stores, supermarkets, grocery shops, local markets and street vendors. It is available pickled, in jars, throughout the year.

In the US and UK, neither the fruit nor the pickled jars are widely available and can only be obtained from Middle Eastern or Arab specialty stores.

Although the almond is often preserved as a dried nut, it cannot be preserved in green almond form.

In its fresh immature form, the fruit is eaten in the Middle East. Louz akhdar is a traditional Levantine snack, that is also eaten in Turkey, Iran and the Arabian Peninsula.

For gastronomic uses, it is often:

1. Eaten raw as a snack, mostly dipped in salt.
2. Pickled to increase its shelf life in its green form.
3. Chopped and used raw in various fresh salads.
4. The main ingredient in a stew where it is cooked with (or without) meat in tomato sauce,

*pickled green almond*

*green almond stew with yogurt*

or yogurt and served with plain rice (or bread if bi zeit). This can be a surprise to many in the Southern Levant, traditional heartlands of the fruit as these recipes are relatively out of favour, but not to many in Turkey or Iran where these recipes continue being enjoyed.
5. Is used as a main vegetable in a pilaf with bulgur or as a maqloubeh version.

## Lift / Turnip

Turnip[15] is a globally cultivated root vegetable and is eaten worldwide. It is white skinned with purple top. While it is common in most countries, it has fallen out of fashion and become undervalued as food. Despite this, it is included here as it is still popular in the Southern Levant and the sight of bright pink pickle is still common in the region.

*turnip vegetable*

In parts of the UK or Canada, the word turnip refers to rutabaga, also known as swede - a larger, yellow root vegetable in the Brassica genus. The Brassica genus includes several well-known vegetables such as kale, cabbage, broccoli, cauliflower, collard greens,

*turnip versus swede*

---

[15] Scientific name is Brassica rapa subsp. rapa

Brussels sprouts, kohlrabi and mustard.

Turnip is common in the Middle East and North Africa, where it is known by the name lift (Arabic: لفت) in most Arab countries including the South Levant. It is known as shalgham (Arabic: شلغم) or shaglam (Arabic: شغلم) in Iraq.

In the Southern Levant turnip, in the form of the root vegetable, is often bought fresh from grocery stores and supermarkets. It can also be bought pickled from most supermarkets and food stores.

In the US and the UK, the fresh vegetable can be found in many grocery stores and supermarkets, but its availability is not common. The pickled variety is available mostly in Middle Eastern and Asian ethnic shops and supermarkets or it can be bought online.

Turnip can be stored frozen at home after being chopped and fried. Although this is not available commercially.

Globally, turnip is a versatile root vegetable that can be eaten raw, boiled, steamed, sautéed, fried, roasted or baked. In the Southern Levant turnip's culinary uses are:

1. Pickled, where it is an ingredient in many sandwiches, or a condiment serves with many

*pickled turnip*

dishes.
2. The main ingredient in certain mahshi recipes, which has numerous recipes with different sauces including versions with yogurt, with tahini, with sumac or with pomegranate molasses.
3. Stewed as the main ingredient or with other vegetables with or without meat.[16]
4. Sliced, chopped or grated raw or sautéed in salads.

*stuffed lift with tahini*

## Turnip leaves and stems

'Turnip Greens' refer specifically to the stem and leafy green part of the turnip plant. Besides the root, both the stems and the leaves of the turnip are edible, but they even get less attention than the root vegetable.

*turnip leaves and root*

It is hard to buy turnip greens separately. They are usually obtained when buying the fresh root vegetable. It is best to keep them attached to the turnip root until usage, otherwise they will wilt quickly. Canned turnip greens are available commercially, but that availability is limited.

Generally, turnip greens are cooked

---

[16] An Iraqi famous stew/soup is called hamid shalqham (Arabic: حامض شلغم), and is getting known in the Southern Levant due to Iraqi refugees waves.

similarly to kale, collard greens and Swiss chard. They can be sautéed, stewed or used in salads.

In the Southern Levant, the leaves have several culinary uses:

1. Stuffed with bulgur or rice, with or without meat, similar to vine leaves.
2. As a filling in pastries, like the famous spinach pastries.
3. Stewed with tomatoes, with or without meat.
4. In salads, as raw green leaf.

*turnip leaves salad*

# Fakkous / Armenian Cucumber

Fakkous is a fresh fruit, treated as culinary vegetable, which is known as Armenian cucumber in English.[17] It is a variety of muskmelon that tastes like and resembles a cucumber on the inside, but with thinner, more pale, green skin. When marketed, it is sometimes erroneously called 'wild cucumber' which is, in fact, a different fruit from the same botanic family.[18] Other English names for the fruit include snake yard-long cucumber, cucumber or snake melon. It should not be confused with snake gourd (Arabic: بدوال), which is a distant relative in the

*wild cucumber*

---

[17] Scientific name is Cucumis melo var. flexuosus.
[18] Wild cucumber is Cucumis anguria.

Cucurbitaceae gourd family (Arabic: الفصيلة القرعية).

The English spellings of the Levantine name are fakkous, faquos or faggous. feggous is the regional version name of the fruit, which has many names in Arabic, while in the Southern Levant, Libya, Tunisia[19] and Morocco, it is called fakkous (Arabic: فقوس). Its name in standard Arabic is qitha' (Arabic: قثاء) or tarh (Arabic: طرح); it is known as khiyar Ta'rouzi (Arabic: خيار طعروزي) in Iraq; fa'ous (Arabic: فئوس) in Egypt; 'ajjour (Arabic) in Sudan and qush'ur (Arabic: قشعر) in Yemen.

It is eaten in the Middle East, North Africa, the Caucasus region and parts of the Indian subcontinent.

In the Southern Levant, fakkous is often bought fresh from grocery stores, supermarkets or even from the backs of trucks or sellers by roadside. It can also be bought pickled from most supermarkets and food stores.

In the US and the UK, the vegetable is still uncommon, being available mainly in ethnic shops and supermarkets, either fresh or pickled (which is also available online).

In the Southern Levant, fakkous is eaten raw when in season. Other

*pickled fakkous*

---

[19] Also known as wild al-qamar (Arabic: ولد القمر)

culinary uses are:

1. Pickled, where it is often marketed under the incorrect wild cucumber name.
2. Chopped or grated in fresh salads.
3. Used as main ingredient in mahshi, which has numerous recipes with different sauces including a version with yogurt.

*stuffed fakkois with yogurt*

## Freekeh / Roasted Cracked Green Wheat

Also spelled as freekah, frikeh or farik (Arabic: فريكة) this is a cereal[20], made from green wheat, particularly durum wheat.[21] It is essentially wheat that has been harvested early, while the grains are still tender and green. The kernels are then parched, roasted, dried and rubbed, sometimes cracked coarsely.

*freekeh cereal*

Nowadays, grains constitute the basis of the Southern Levantine cuisine, with rice, and wheat-based bread eaten at almost every meal. Before rice became the dominant grain eaten in the Southern Levant, the cuisine was dominated by several types of various

---

[20] A cereal is any grass cultivated (grown) for the edible components of its grain, composed of the endosperm, germ, and bran. The term may also refer to the resulting grain itself (specifically 'cereal grain'). https://en.wikipedia.org/wiki/Cereal

[21] Scientific name is Triticum turgidum var. durum

sized groats,[22] most of which are derivatives of wheat. The main types are bulgur (Arabic: برغل), cracked wheat 'Jaressh' (Arabic: جريش), freekeh and wheat berry (Arabic: قمح مقشور).

Apart from freekeh, the difference between the other wheat products is that bulgur is precooked, dried and cracked, then ground to various degrees (fine, medium, coarse and extra coarse), whereas jareesh is not precooked before being ground. Wheat berries are not cracked but instead are hulled and used whole. All these methods were used historically to preserve grains, but nowadays the methods are used for specific gastronomic reasons.

In Southern Levant, freekeh is available at supermarkets, grocery shops, local markets, farms and other traditional suppliers. It can be bought in bulk or pre-packaged.

In the US and UK, freekeh is still fairly unknown, unlike bulgur and jareesh (cracked wheat), which made it to mainstream supermarket shelves and is just starting to be recognised as a superfood, rivalling quinoa in the US and the UK. It can be increasingly found

*packaged freekeh*

---

[22] Groats, are the hulled kernels of various cereal grains such as oat, wheat, and rye. Groats are whole grains that include the cereal germ and fiber-rich bran portion of the grain as well as the endosperm. Groats can also be produced from pseudocereal seeds such as buckwheat
https://educalingo.com/en/dic-en/groats

in supermarkets and some grocery stores. It can also be obtained from Middle Eastern or Arab specialty stores. It can also be found online.

Just to clarify any confusion, note that couscous, a staple in Maghreb countries (also becoming widespread worldwide) is actually a pasta made of semolina.[23] Hand-made maftoul or moghrabieh, known in English as giant couscous, is based on bulgur, rather than semolina and is the 'cousin' of couscous' in the Levant, while factory-made maftoul is simply a dried pasta.

*maftoul or moahrabieh*

In the Southern Levant freekeh has numerous culinary uses including:

1. As a very versatile grain, freekeh can be an alternative to rice, bulgur, jareesh, wheat berries or even quinoa, or any of the other ancient grains in almost any recipe. Examples include in mahsi or as pilaf. There are recipes online that are using freekeh in kibbeh, kufta, salads and tabbouleh. The most famous dish is mansaf freekeh, made from cooked freekeh, topped with meat or poultry and spices then topped with fried or roasted nuts.
2. As a main ingredient in soup,

*mansaf freekeh*

*freekeh soup*

---

[23] Semolina and flour are made by grinding raw grains, the former is coarse, while the latter is powder.

mostly chicken based.
3. Eaten fresh when hot by kids as a snack.

# Summaq / Sumac

Sumac (Arabic: سماق), also spelled as summaq, sumaq, sumak, sumach, soumak (amongst many variations), is a spice with tangy sour taste. It is widely used in the Middle East, North Africa, as well as recipes in the Central and South Asian cuisines. The spice comes from the crushed dried fruit of a variety of the sumac tree or shrub, native to southern Europe and Western Asia.[24] The word originally comes from Aramaic summāqā 'red', via Arabic, Latin and French.[25]

*sumac tree*

In addition to its culinary uses, the plant has medicinal and industrial properties, particularly in the tanning industry, where it has been used for centuries. It can also be used as an ornamental plant.

*Sumac berries*

Currently sumac can be found as a crushed dried spice and the berries can be bought loose from deli-type counters in Southern Levant supermarkets, speciality shops, spice merchants, or readily pre-packaged off the shelves.

*crushed sumac spice*

---

[24] Scientific name is Rhus coriaria
[25] Oxford English Dictionary, 3rd edition

Similarly, in most of the US and UK, loose or pre-packaged forms can be bought from mainstream grocery shops, supermarkets and from many ethnic shops. It is also available at many online stores worldwide or can arrive at your front door via delivery apps.

The fresh berries can also be used as tea. Nowadays several brands of teabags of sumac berries are available.

In North America, sumac berries are sometimes used to make a fizzy beverage called 'sumac-ade', which tastes like lemonade. Some Native Americans combine sumac leaves and fruits with tobacco for traditional smoking mixtures.

The reddish-purple powdery spice is strongly present in Middle Eastern cuisines, adding a tarty, sour, lemony flavour to salads and meat. In Southern Levant cuisine, it is used as:

1. A garnish on appetisers such as hummus, mutabbal and other meze dishes.
2. Added as a spice in sauces, or with onion, or tahini, to accompany popular sandwiches such as shawarma and falafel.
3. An important seasoning in many poultry, meat (including kebabs and kibbeh) and fish dishes.
4. An important seasoning in some

rice dishes.
5. As a topping and filling for many pastry dishes such as fatayer spinach and sfeeha.
6. Added to salads. One famous example is fattoush, which is a salad made from pieces of Arabic bread (khubz, sometimes toasted or fried) combined with mixed greens and other vegetables such as tomatoes, cucumbers, onions and radishes.
7. An important ingredient in zaatar (see above).
8. As a main ingredient in musakhan, the traditional Palestinian dish, which is made of sumac, chicken, onion and olive oil over taboon flat bread.

*musakhan*

9. As a main ingredient in summaqiya, which is a speciality of the Gaza Strip, made of sumac and tahini, with sautéed diced onion, chopped chard, pieces of stewed lamb and chickpeas with dill. Note that a related vegetarian version of the dish, kibbeh summaqiya, is popular in Northern Syria in Aleppo, where lamb meat is substituted by kibbeh.

*summaqiya*

10. As a sour syrup called dibis sumac (Arabic: دبس سماق).

*dibis sumac*

# Jameed

Jameed (Arabic: جميد), is a traditional dairy product of Bedouin origin, made mainly from sheep's milk, although goat, cow and camel milk are sometimes used. The word 'jameed' is the most well-known form of terminology for the product in Western Asia and worldwide, but in many regions, other names are used such as 'marees' (Arabic: مريس), 'aqt' (Arabic: أقط), 'kathi' (Arabic: كثي) or 'jathi' (Arabic: جثي).

*jameed balls*

In the West 'jameed' is sometimes referred to as 'rock cheese'.

Traditionally, making jameed was a preservation process that took several days. In the spring and summer, the plentiful milk is firstly transformed into a thick yogurt, which is then shaken in specialised leather bags, made from sheep or goat leather, to separate the butter. The leftover buttermilk, called makheedh (Arabic: مخيض) or shanineh (Arabic: شنينة), is then reduced first by boiling, then by adding some salt, until it reaches a thick consistency. It is placed in a special cloth to drain out excess whey, until it has a consistency like labaneh (see next section). It is salted, shaped into balls and dried naturally, removing any moisture, until it turns a yellow or white colour. The colour of the jameed depends on whether the drying process is carried out in the sun or in the shade. These dry cheeseballs are preserved for months.

Currently, several steps of this process have been mechanised, with mixers and food processors replacing traditional leather bags, etc.

Nowadays, people enjoy eating jameed for its flavour rather than the necessity of preservation methods. Due to the involved process of making it, jameed is often bought in its dried balls form. However, to prepare it for cooking, it needs to be rehydrated from powdered, in quite a labour-intensive process.

Recently several companies have started offering Jameed in a ready-to-use liquid form and like bouillon/stock cubes, as a dried powder form.

*jameed cubes*

In Southern Levant, jameed is available at supermarkets, grocery shops, local markets, farms and other traditional suppliers. It can be found in the traditional form or as a liquid, in cartons, bottles, jars or cans, as well as the stock-cube-like boxes.

In the US and UK, jameed is still rare and can only be obtained from Middle Eastern or Arab specialty stores. Also, it can be bought online.

Jameed is considered a cornerstone of Jordanian cuisine but is widely used in

*ready liquid jameed*

the rest of the Levant, Iraq and the Arabian Peninsula. It is also used to a lesser extent in the rest of Western and Central Asia.

Jameed usage is seen in numerous recipes and also can be used instead of yogurt in many recipes. Amongst the most famous recipes are:

1. Mansaf, which is the traditional dish of Jordan. It is a Jordanian lamb stew, made of lamb cooked in a sauce of jameed, spices and served with rice (regional varieties can use jareesh or bulgur). Variations can use chicken instead of lamb but they are not held in the same esteem.

*mansaf*

2. Rashouf, which is a thick soup/porridge dish made of lentils, jareesh or bulgur, jameed, sometimes chickpea, topped with fried onion and samneh. It is served with sour pickles and vegetables.
3. In dolmas (mahshis) such as courgette/zucchini mahshi as a substitute for yogurt.
4. In stews such as fava beans stew, cauliflower stew, etc. Also, as a substitute for yogurt.
5. With kibbeh (and kuftas) and shishbarak, as a substitute for yogurt
6. Served with tripe.

7. Grated over and/or added to soup.
8. Recently creatively used in chocolates, or ice creams.

Two dairy products are sometimes confused in people's minds with jameed or labaneh, depending on the way they look or are produced. These are shanklessh and kishk.

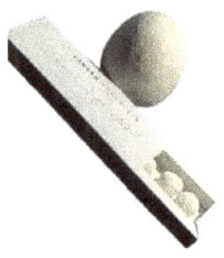

*chocolate jameed*

*jameed ice cream*

## Shankleesh

Also spelled as chancliche and shinklish (Arabic: شنكليش), this is a traditional North Levantine cheese, which is the Levantine equivalent to blue cheese. It can be made from sheep, goat or cow's milk. It is formed into cheese balls with an off-white interior, coated with spices, often with zaatar or red pepper (Aleppo pepper). It is known as sorke, or sürke in Turkey.

*shankleesh balls*

Shankleesh is traditionally made in Northern Levant. The traditional method is like the way jameed is made (see above), but the difference is that once the leftover buttermilk reaches the labaneh consistency, salt and spices are then added and the mixture is formed into small balls, which are often covered in zaatar and red pepper (sometimes curd yogurt or fresh labaneh is fermented and used instead). It is then dried for several days. At that point it can be stored in the fridge ready to eat or can be aged (to mature for longer) by placing the balls in air-tight/sealed jars, preferably in the dark. The outer layer will begin to mould and develop rots, in the same way that blue cheese is aged. The mould is removed by placing the balls in very hot water for some time before rinsing them. The resultant is a cheese with a hard consistency.

Shankleesh varies greatly in its texture and flavour, depending on the length of drying time and 'fungus growth', where it becomes progressively harder, acquiring a strong pungent odour. The flavour intensifies, becoming sharper with age.

Traditionally, shankleesh was made as a form of preserving cheese, but nowadays it is made for its particular taste and is a desired food ingredient. It is often preserved in vegetable oil.

*fresh shankleesh*

In the Southern Levant, although not particularly popular in the region, shankleesh can be found in supermarkets and grocery stores.

In the US and UK, it is not available at mainstream shops, but can be found at Middle Eastern food stores.

*shankleesh in oil*

In the Southern Levant, shankleesh has several culinary uses such as:

1. Eaten with finely-chopped tomato, onion, parsley, and olive oil – often as part of several mezza or appetizer dishes.
2. Crushed in flat bread with cucumbers, mint, and olive oil for breakfast.
3. As an ingredient in several fresh salads.
4. As a topping on manaqeesh and recently on pizza.
5. As a flavouring ingredient mashed up with boiled eggs, or part of fried eggs or ijjeh.

*shankleesh salad*

## Kishk

This is also spelled as keshk, keshek, kashk (Arabic: كشك). It is a dairy product in the Levant, made from cereals and combined with curdled milk. The same name is used in other parts of the world, where it can refer to a range of dairy products based on curdled milk products like yogurt or cheese, as well as foods based on wheat, barley, bread or flour and broth or soup (often in Persian and Tajik cuisine).

*bulk kishk*

Famous for centuries in Persia, kishk is also a traditional food in Western Asia, the Caucasus, Central Asia, parts of the Indian subcontinent and Mongolia.

This large geographical footprint has resulted in many names being given to the same product including qurut and chortan.

Irrespective of the exact recipe, it is commonly made from drained yogurt or sour milk, which is then shaped and allowed to dry. It is then formed into a variety of shapes - rolled into balls, sliced into strips, shaped into discs and chunks or powdered.

*traditional West Asian kashk*

In Southern Levant, the variety of kishk is made using similar methods to that of jameed (see above), but instead, once the leftover buttermilk reaches the labaneh consistency, it is mixed with bulgur, salted and fermented for several days (sometimes curdled yogurt and/or labaneh can be used instead of, or with, the leftover buttermilk). It is kneaded regularly, allowed to dry and then formed into shapes or rubbed well, until it is reduced to a powder.

*kishk discs*

Kishk can be eaten prior to the fermentation process where it is called green kishk (Arabic: كشك أخضر, referring to fresh kishk). As with other dairy produce, kishk was made as a way to preserve food and avoid it spoiling but, these days it is made for its taste as it has become a desired food ingredient.

In the Southern Levant, kishk can be found at mainstream supermarkets and grocery stores in the fresh produce

*packaged kishk*

section. It is available commercially in jars, cartons and plastic bags, as well as being sold loose/bulk.

In the US and the UK, Levantine kishk is not available at mainstream supermarkets and grocery stores. It can be found in Middle Eastern ethnic shops. Also, it can be obtained online. Other namesake kishk from other cuisines can be found at different ethnic shops.

In the Southern Levant kishk has several culinary uses such as:

1. As a dish called kishkia, added to a mixture of boiled bulgur, jareesh, chickpeas, lentils, sometimes jameed and yogurt. This is cooked to porridge-like consistency, then it is topped with fried diced garlic.
2. As a filling with sautéed onion in fatayer or topping in manakeesh
3. Boiled with bulgur and tomatoes.
4. Added to sautéed diced onion then boiled.
5. Added to pilaf rice with boiled shredded chicken and chickpea, dill and red pepper, then cooked in chicken stock to porridge consistency, then topped with fried diced onion and garlic.
6. As substitute to jameed in rashouf.
7. As a soup with garlic and

*kishkia*

sometimes gourd. Boiled chicken or kibbeh can be added to the soup and cooked.
8. As a filling in kibbeh

# Labaneh / Strained Yogurt

Also spelled as labneh (Arabic: لبنة), this is yogurt that has been strained to remove most of its whey. Sheep, cow and goat's yogurt can be used. It is historically another preservation process for yogurt, that now become popular in its own right. It can be considered as a type of white soft cream cheese.

*labaneh*

Alongside zaatar, this is an indispensable staple food in Jordanian and Palestinian cuisine.

Labaneh, technically thick yogurt, is used fresh, slightly salted or strongly salted, it can have herbs (e.g. oregano) added, it can be shaped into balls and sun-dried, then stored in olive oil (commercial versions use other vegetables oils).

*Labaneh muka'baleh*

There are analogous Western versions of labaneh, but they are often creamier, milder and sweeter. Some types of Welsh goat's cheese have a very similar texture and taste.

As discussed in the previous section,

labaneh can be used as an alternative ingredient when making shankleesh or kishk.

In the Southern Levant, labaneh can be found at all supermarkets and grocery stores. It is available as fresh dairy product or in a preserved form as hard balls in oil. It can also be obtained fresh from farmers directly.

*pre-packaged fresh labaneh*

In the US and the UK, labaneh can be found at some supermarkets and grocery stores, as well as many ethnic food stores. It can also be obtained online.

*labaneh balls in oil*

Labaneh is very popular food in the Southern Levant. It can be eaten in many ways including:

1. As a spread in sandwiches on its own, with mint, zaatar or mortadella, etc.
2. As mezza with olive oil and some garnish
3. As a topping on manaqueesh.
4. As a filling in fatayer.
5. As an ingredient in ijjeh.
6. The main ingredient in some soups.
7. Mixed with pomegranate or with beetroot as a mezza.
8. As an ingredient in some fresh salads.

*labaneh as mezza*

Recently chefs are experimenting with it in different ways, like:

1. An ingredient in pickled vegetables, stuffed with labaneh.
2. In aubergine/eggplant stew.
3. In labaneh and green olive qatayef.

# Nabulsi Cheese

Nabulsi Cheese is a type of cheese-in-brine, originating from the city of Nablus in the West Bank. It is a white semi-hard cheese made, originally from sheep milk and occasionally from goat milk or a mixture of both. Recently commercial versions are made with cow's milk. The cheese is often boiled in salty water to preserve it. Nigella seeds are usually added to it after boiling. When boiling, the cheese is flavoured by adding mastic[26] and mahlab[27] to the boiling salty water. After boiling, Nabulsi Cheese can be stored in the freezer or in airtight brine.

*Nabulsi cheese*

Several other types of other white cheeses-in-brine are popular in the Southern Levant. These include Akkawi Cheese, which originated in the city of Acre and Halloumi Cheese, which originated in Cyprus.

---

[26] Scientific name is Pistacia lentiscus, an aromatic resin from the mastic tree – see Butum Section
[27] Scientific name is Prunus mahaleb, an aromatic spice made from the seeds of the fruits of St Lucie cherry, a species of the cherry tree.

These traditional cheeses are an essential part of local life and cuisine. The Levant is having a resurgence of appreciation in the preserving of local culinary history, traditions and culture of the entire region.

In the Southern Levant, Nabulsi cheese can be found at grocery stores and supermarkets. It can also be bought from specialised dairy shops or directly from farmers, who often sell it fresh (not boiled) in a softer form referred to as 'green cheese' and it needs boiling prior to storing it.

*pre-pakaged Nabulsi cheese*

Halloumi cheese is already a mainstream cheese in the West and can be bought at any supermarket or grocery shop, whereas Nabulsi and Akkawi cheeses are only available in specialized ethnic shops.

This white cheese is very popular in Southern Levant cuisines, where it is used as:

1. Alone, as part of breakfast meals with bread.
2. A filling in sandwiches.
3. Added to salads.
4. Paired with fruits (watermelon, grapes, figs).
5. Fried.
6. Chopped and added to omelettes or scrambled eggs.
7. Grilled, similar to Halloumi

*fried Nabulsi cheese*

grilled cheese, which is becoming popular in the US and UK.
8. As a topping or filling, in pastries, especially mixed with parsley, oregano, thyme, mint or other green herbs.
9. De-salted then used as a base for the famous dessert kunafa Nabulsia, which is the main dessert in both Palestine and Jordan. Note, the Gazan variety does not include cheese.

*kunafa Nabulsia*

10. De-salted then used as a filling in qatayef, which is a special pancake dessert eaten in Ramadan.

*qatayef*

11. Kullaj, a Palestinian dessert similar to baklava, except it is served hot and can be stuffed with sweet cheese instead of nuts.

*kullaj*

Note, when used in desserts, the cheese must be desalted. Also, Akkawi cheese, which is milder, is often used as a substitute.

Recently several recipes appeared using Nabulsi cheese in pizza or with zaatar/oregano as a salt cake, but with traditional cake recipe.

# Part II

# Disappearing Ingredients

Here we turn our focus towards ingredients whose popular usage is becoming rarer, are less well-known, or even unknown, to many in the Southern Levant, despite previously being common or even ubiquitous.

Most of the ingredients covered in Part 2 are found rarely in the UK and the US. While the ingredients covered in Part I can be found relatively easily in these countries, either having become mainstream in grocery stores, supermarkets and in many ethnic shops, the ingredients in Part 2 are more difficult to find. Indeed, it is becoming increasingly difficult to obtain some of them, even in the Southern Levant.

One common factor with all the foods in this section is that they are not being farmed commercially. The plants are found seasonally, in the wild and are eaten now mostly by older generations. Several cultural revival projects and campaigns in the Southern Levant have led to something of a revival for these once popular items, which are now being re-introduced to younger generations.

In this section I will present many plants, which, in my opinion, have great culinary value and should be celebrated. There are a multitude of plants that I could have included but, for our purposes, I have deliberately selected only those which are ultimately used as ingredients in various recipes. There are numerous plants, particularly leafy vegetables, described here but the following pages are a selection, rather than a comprehensive guide, of all these old-fashioned ingredients.

To be honest, growing up in an affluent neighbourhood in Amman, I too was unfamiliar with many of the plants listed below. I may have heard about some of them from my grandmothers, but I had never used them myself. I discovered most of these ingredients once I started researching this book. Many in the Southern Levant will relate to my experience and, hopefully when they learn about them here, will become just as enthusiastic as I have.

## Kama'a / Desert Truffle

Strictly speaking, Kama'a (Arabic: كمأة) is a fungus not a vegetable, however for culinary purposes, it is like a vegetable. The fungus, known as desert truffle or terfeziaceae[28], is labelled truffle as it grows underground, like those of the highly prized European truffle family, which cannot be cultivated, hence leading to their expensive price. In the

*Kama'a fungus*

---

[28] Scientific names for the genera are Terfezia, Tirmania and Mattirolomyces that include over 30 species.

past, some of these truffles have been sold for over US$100,00 per kilo.[29]

Desert truffle also cannot be cultivated, and thus it is very expensive ingredient in the Middle East, it is considerably cheaper that the extremely expensive European varieties.

Kama'a has a variety of names in Arabic including terfas (Arabic: ترفاس), kema (Arabic: كما), and fuqu' or fugu' (Arabic: فقع).

In the Southern Levant, kama'a is available fresh when in season or in grocery stores and supermarkets all year round, preserved in cans and jars.

*Canned kama'a*

In the UK and the US, desert truffle is rarely available fresh at mainstream grocery shops or supermarkets. It can be found at speciality or ethnic shops especially in cans and jars.

Kama'a can also be stored dried or frozen (at home), either whole or sliced, for up to a year. No frozen kama'a packs are available commercially. For short term storage, kama'a can be preserved in rice or olive oil for up to two weeks. Note this can affect the gastronomic quality and taste.

In the Southern Levant the kama'a has

---

[29] https://worthly.com/most-expensive/food-spirits/most-expensive-truffles/

several culinary uses:

1. Sautéed with diced onion and olive oil.
2. Served as above with egg.
3. Stewed with meat and onion, and sometimes jameed.
4. As a main ingredient in maqloubeh with rice, bulgur and other rice mixed dishes (e,g. kabsa).
5. Grilled on skewers.
6. Recently being used as a substitute for other mushrooms in pasta dishes or as a pizza topping.

*stewed kama'a*

# Hummedha / Sorrel or Dock

Most people around the world, are familiar with hummedha or hummedh (Arabic: حميض or حميضة), a leafy plant, known in English as sorrel or dock, that is part of the 'Genus Rumex'. This is an umbrella term that includes over 200 species, many of which are edible and have various culinary uses in many cuisines around the globe. They are used (often as herbs) in salads, soups and stews or incorporated into pasta dishes.

*hummedha plant*

In the Southern Levant, several species of rumex are edible and the leaves are collected for use as food. The popular types in the region are often referred to under one encompassing name, although as stated before, there are several distinct botanical species.[30]

In the Southern Levant, if you cannot forage or harvest hummedha yourself, in season, you can buy them from street and roadside vendors.

In the West, hummedha is sometimes available from specialist Middle Eastern shops or farmers markets, although the variety available may not be the one you are expecting[31].

As with other green leafy vegetables, coarsely chopped hummedha can be stored frozen (at home) either after blanching or directly from fresh, by going through a pre-freezing process first. Frozen hummedha leaves are not available in packs commercially. It can also be coarsely chopped and cold stored in jars in its own juice, in cold water or in brine.

Hummedha can be dried for use as a herb.

In the Southern Levant, hummedha leaves and stalks have numerous culinary uses:

---

[30] Scientific names are Rumex cyprius Murb., Rumex vesicarius L., Rumex occultans Sam.
[31] Most common varieties are Rumex acetosa, Rumex patientia, Rumex acetosella and Rumex scutatus.

1. Eaten raw, finely chopped in salad with diced onion, lemon juice, olive oil and salt.
2. Sautéed with diced onion and olive oil, eaten with flat bread.
3. Stewed with diced onion and lentils.
4. As main filling with onion in fatayer (pastry parcels) similar to the famous spinach fatayer.
5. Stuffed with spiced rice with or without minced meat similar to vine leaves.
6. Stewed with minced meat and yogurt.

*hummedha fatayer*

In the Levant, there is another plant sometimes referred to locally as hummedha, but is local type of oxalis (Arabic: أقصليس).32 It too can be eaten in salads or used as fatayer filling and it can be stored in similar fashion to hummedha.

*oxalis plant*

Interestingly, the name sorrel is used for an entirely different plant in the Caribbean, especially Jamaica, where it refers to the roselle plant,33 which is known as karkadeh (Arabic: كركديه), in the Eastern Mediterranean. A chilled drink, infused from roselle flowers, is an integral part of traditional engagement rituals in Egypt.

*oxalis plant*

---

32 Scientific name is Oxalis pes-caprae and Oxalis corniculate.
33 Scientific name is Hibiscus sabdariffa.

# Hamasees / Rumex Pictus

Hamasses[34] (Arabic: حمصيص) is a leafy plant also part of the rumex genus discussed in the previous section. This particular species is native to the Eastern Mediterranean, where the leaves are gathered as a food ingredient. It is very popular in Gaza as a main ingredient in a traditional winter dish listed below.

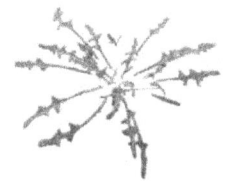

*hamasees plant*

In the Southern Levant, hamasees leaves are sometimes available at mainstream grocery stores or supermarkets, when in season. They can also be obtained in season from street and roadside vendors who collect and sell them.

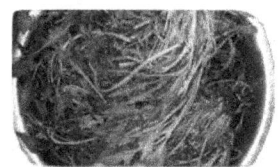

*hamasees leaves*

In the US and the UK, the leaves are not available commercially, unlike their cousins. sorrels or docks, which are often available at mainstream supermarkets or grocery stores. They may be found at some farmers markets.

Similar to other green leafy vegetables, coarsely chopped hamasses leaves can be frozen at home, either after blanching or directly from fresh after going through a pre-freezing process.

In the Southern Levant, hamasees is a speciality of Gaza and Sinai, where the leaves are used as:

---

[34] Scientific name is Rumex pictus Forssk.

1. Stewed with boiled lentils and eaten with flat bread.
2. As main filling with onion and sumac in fatayer (pastry parcels) like the famous spinach fatayer.

*Gazan hamasees*

Be aware that in the Northern Levant, the oxalis plant (discussed in the previous section) is sometimes referred to as hamasees.

# Lsaineh / Jerusalem Salvia

Lsaineh[35] (Arabic: لسينة) is found throughout the Levant and Cyprus. However its name, both commonly and scientifically, is often confused with those other plants. Commonly it is known as Jerusalem salvia and Jerusalem sage, but the latter name is sometimes applied to another plant from the Sage family, phlomis fruticose.

*lsaineh plant*

Adding to the potential confusion, on the internet, when translated from Arabic, the plant is often erroneously referred to as a type of borage plant,[36] which is yet another edible leafy plant, popular in Spain.

*lsaineh leaves*

In Arabic, the plant has different names including ورق اللسان and lisan al-thawr

---

[35] Scientific name is Salvia hierosolymitana.
[36] Scientific name Borago officinalis L.

(Arabic: لسان الثور). The latter name is also sometimes found used for another plant (as discussed below).

Like khubeiza, the plant grows wild and is abundant when in season. Its footprint now extends globally. Very limited attempts are made to commercially cultivate it.

In the Southern Levant, the vegetable is available in mainstream outlets at supermarkets, grocery stores and from roadside vendors, when in season. It is also abundant as wild plant.

In the US or the UK, it is hard to obtain the vegetable as it is not available at mainstream outlets. It can sometimes be found in ethnic shops or at farmers markets. It is sometimes listed on online outlets. Certainly, keen people can still collect it in the wild.

As with other green leafy vegetables, lsaineh leaves can be stored frozen either after blanching, or directly from fresh by going through a pre-freezing process first. Frozen lsaineh leaves are not available in packs commercially.

In the Southern Levant the plant's leaves main culinary use is:

1. Stuffed with bulgur, rice or freekeh, with or without meat, similar to vine leaves.

*stuffed lsaineh*

Another related plant, anchusa,[37] known as the Common bugloss or alkanet, is sometimes also called 'lisan al-thawr', translated as ox tongue in Arabic, especially in Northern Levant. It is edible there, the leaves are sautéed, with oil and onion, or with egg as ijjeh. The leaves and young shoots can be cooked like spinach, while the flowers are used as a garnish.

*lisan al-thawr plant*

## Waraq Toot / Mulberry Leaves

The familiar Mulberry tree (Arabic: توت, pronounced toot) is known worldwide. The cultivated varieties differ by the colour of their fruits - white, red, and black mulberries.[38]

*mulberry leaves and fruits*

While the fruits are an important crop consumed fresh or made into jams, sherbets, juices or dried, the trees are even more famous for their leaves. Mulberry leaves are used to feed silkworms in the commercial production of silk.

Our main interest is only in talking about mulberry leaves (Arabic: ورق توت, pronounced waraq toot) and their culinary purposes. This usage is common mainly in parts of the Eastern

---

[37] Scientific name Anchusa officinalis L.
[38] Scientific names are Morus alba, Morus rubra, and Morus nigra

Mediterranean.

In the Southern Levant, mulberry leaves are not common at mainstream grocery stores or supermarkets. They can sometimes be bought fresh from some grocery stores if in season, or from farmers outlets.

In the US and the UK, mulberry leaves are not available in the fresh form at mainstream grocery stores or supermarkets, but can be found at specialised organic stores and at farmers markets. Dried leaves can be bought from grocery and health stores or online.

As with other green leafy vegetables, mulberry leaves can be stored frozen either after blanching, or directly from fresh by going through a pre-freezing process first. Frozen mulberry leaves are not available in packaged form commercially.

In the Southern Levant there are several ways mulberry leaves and shoots are used:

1. Stuffed with bulgur, rice or jareesh (cracked wheat), with or without meat, similar to vine leaves.
2. Stuffed with chicken or lamb.
3. The young shoots can be sautéed in oil.

*Stuffed mulberry leaves*

# Zamatout / Cyclamen Leaves

Zamatout (Arabic: زعمطوط), known as Cyclamen in English.[39] This is a familiar flowering plant that grows from tubers. It is a common plant that has many local names such as sowbread or swinebread.

*cyclamen plant*

In Arabic the plant has various names, which, besides zamatout, include nine others: rakaf or rakafa (Arabic: ركف or ركفة), bukhour Mariam (Arabic: بخور مريم), qarn al-ghazal (Arabic: قرن الغزال), 'asa al-ra'ii (Arabic: عصا الراعي), daghnineh (Arabic: دغنينة), troughanineh (Arabic: تروغنينة), sakouka' (Arabic: سكوكع) and 'artanitha (Arabic: عرطنيثا).

Zamatout is well-known as an ornamental plant, appreciated for its beautiful flowers and patterned leaves in the Western world. In the Levant, most people consider it a hardy garden or wild plant. However, while the plant's leaves are edible, the flowers and roots are not.

In the Southern Levant, the zamatout plant can be bought from florists and garden centres.

---

[39] Scientific name is Cyclamen L.

As a food ingredient, it can be bought fresh, in season, from grocery stores and supermarkets, or from farmers outlets.

In the US and the UK, the plant is also available at florists and garden centres. It is not available as a food ingredient (maybe at some farmers markets). Keen chefs could perhaps grow it in their herb gardens.

As with other green leafy vegetables, zamatout can be stored by freezing it at home either after blanching, or directly from fresh by going through a pre-freezing process first. Frozen zamatout leaves are not available commercially.

In the Southern Levant the plant's leaves have culinary uses similar to lsaineh:

1. Stuffed with bulgur, rice or jareesh (cracked wheat), with or without meat, similar to vine leaves.

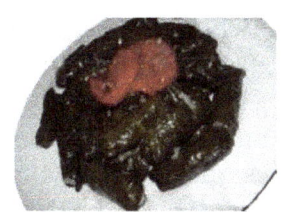

*stuffed zamatout*

Important note - although some internet sites[40] suggest that tubers can be eaten after deep frying to remove their poisonous effects this is, in fact, not advised.

---

[40] https://ar.wikipedia.org/wiki/%D8%A8%D8%AE%D9%88%D8%B1_%D9%85%D8%B1%D9%8A%D9%85

75

# Lakhneh / Cauliflower Leaves

In the Southern Levant, lakneh (Arabic: لخنة) is the name given to cauliflower leaves. Cauliflower[41] is a vegetable known across the globe. For most people, the edible part of the plant is the head, called the curd, which is composed of clusters of flower buds or florets, mostly white, but some varieties are green, yellow, orange or purple.[42] However, besides the head, cauliflower leaves and stems are also edible. The plant is part of the Brassicaceae family. The Cauliflowers closest relatives are cabbage, broccoli, kale, Brussels sprouts, collard greens and kohlrabi.

*cauliflower plant*

*lakhneh leaves*

While most people discard cauliflower leaves, they are in fact nutritious and can be used as substitute for more common leaves from similar green vegetables like collard greens and kale. In the past, the leaves were a common culinary ingredient in the Southern Levant, but their popularity is diminishing. In contrast, the leaves are becoming increasingly popular with chefs in the US and Europe as part of the healthy living trend which is constantly gaining momentum.

In Arabic, lakneh leaves can also be referred to as waraq zahra (Arabic: ورق زهرة), waraq qarnabeet (Arabic: ورق

---

[41] Scientific name is Brassica oleracea var. botrytis.
[42] Romanesco broccoli is a variation of cauliflower also.

قرنبيط), waraq shoul (Arabic: ورق شول) and waraq tanquibeh (Arabic: ورق تنقيبة).

In the cities of Salt in Jordan and Nablus in Palestine, lakhneh is the name given to the smaller leaf headless cauliflower plants, which only produces leaves.

In the Southern Levant, lakneh is often bought fresh from some grocery stores and supermarkets if in season, or from farmers outlets.

In the US and the UK, cauliflower leaves are not available in the fresh form at mainstream grocery stores and supermarkets, but they can be found in specialised organic stores or some farmers markets.

As with other green leafy vegetables, lakneh can be stored frozen either after blanching, or directly from fresh by going through a pre-freezing process first. Frozen lakneh is not available commercially.

In popular modern cuisine, numerous recipes can be found on the internet using this vegetable in salads, soups, curries, stir fried, sautéed or roasted. In the Southern Levant, lakhneh continues to have traditional culinary uses, which are described in many cookbooks and on the internet:

    1. Stuffed with bulgur, rice or

jareesh (cracked wheat), with or without meat, like vine leaves.
2. Chopped and sautéed with onion, olive oil, garlic and salt.
3. Stewed with onion, garlic and minced meat.
4. Eaten raw, chopped into a salad with onion, garlic, tomatoes, olive oil and vinegar.
5. Eaten as a side dish - cauliflower stems can be sautéed in olive oil with fresh coriander, garlic and lemon juice.

*stuffed lakhneh*

Note that in Northern Levant, the word lakhneh is used to describe cabbage leaves instead of cauliflower leaves, so be sure of what it is that you are buying as it will make a big difference to the flavour of your dish.

Although not labelled as lakhneh, broccoli leaves can be used in similar way to cauliflower leaves. Moreover, collard greens or mustard leaves can be used as substitutes for lakhneh if you want to try the Southern Levantine traditional recipe.

# Loof / Black Calla

Loof (Arabic: لوف) is a flowering plant native to the Eastern Mediterranean but, which is also found in many other regions. It is known as black calla,[43] Solomon's lily, priest's hood, Noo'ah loof and kardi. It is a popular ornamental plant in the West with many medicinal uses. The edible part is the leaves, and it has been eaten for millennia in the Levant.

*loof plant*

In Arabic, the plant has many names besides loof, these include uzun al-fil (Arabic: أذن الفيل, translated elephant's ears) and sam al-hayyeh (Arabic: سم الحية, translated as snake's poison). The name loof is used interchangeably with that of another plant, irgeita (Arabic: إرقيطة or رقيطة) so understandably, many people are confused about which plant is which. However, from a botanical perspective, they are two different species that are closely related; the latter has spotted stem and is discussed in the next section.

*loof flower*

Another plant it is often confused with is biaum pyrami, which is distantly related in the Araceae family.

Surprisingly, despite its long usage as an edible ingredient, the roots, stems, flowers, berries and leaves of loof are poisonous. Despite this, Levantines eat the leaves (but not other parts) after treating them. This is done by drying them, rubbing them with salt and pressing, to get rid of the poisonous elements. It is recommended that the

***Biarum pyramid plant***

---

[43] Scientific name is Arum palaestinum.

leaves are brought to the boil then the water is changed three times for loof and twice for irgeita. (See next section).

Eaten raw, the leaves cause mucous membrane irritation and burning. The consumption of larger doses causes nausea, diarrhoea and cramping. Moreover, exposure to the skin can cause irritation. Even after the preparation treatment described above, eating the leaves can cause some numbness.

In the West, like zamatout, the plant is well-known as an ornamental plant, appreciated for its beautiful flowers and patterned leaves. Similarly, most people in the Levant consider it as hardy garden or wild plant.

In the Southern Levant the black calla plant can be bought from florists and garden centres. As a food ingredient it is often bought fresh from some grocery stores and supermarkets if in season, or from street and roadside vendors and farmers outlets.

In the US and the UK, the plant is available at florists and garden centres. It is not available as a food ingredient (maybe at some farmers markets). A keen chef could consider growing it.

As with other green leafy vegetables, loof can be stored frozen either after blanching, or directly from fresh by going through a pre-freezing process first. Frozen loof leaves are not available commercially.

Loof has many culinary uses in the Southern Levant, which include:

1. Boiled and pressed, then sautéed with onion, olive oil and salt. One can also add lentils in some recipes and boil. Sometimes served added to shredded bread.
2. As above but with egg either as aqras, ijjeh or mufarrakeh and can add sumac.
3. Cut into pieces and boiled in water with the addition of olive oil. Some also add chickpeas to the cooking. After several hours, sumac is also added. It is often served with cooked bulgur wheat.
4. Sautéed with onion, then both boiled with water and adding a handful of rice till cooked.
5. As a filling in fatayer.
6. In cha'acheel, dumplings made of flour, eggs, onion and loof, cooked in boiled jameed (and lentils).
7. As an ingredient is rashouf, which is a thick soup/porridge dish, made of lentils, jareesh or bulgur, jameed, sometimes chickpea, topped with fried

*cooked loof on bread*

onion and samneh. It is served with sour pickles and vegetables.
8. In bahboutha, where it is cooked with dough.
9. As a filling with onion in shushbarak, similar to ravioli.
10. The leaves can also be dried whole. and then chopped or ground and used as a herb.

*bahboutha*

In all the above methods the poisonous leaves are treated first to ensure they are safe to consume.

Note that another plant species, arisarum (Arabic: صرين) looks quite, similar to arum, but its flowers, spathes and inflorescences are considerably different.

*arisarum plant*

# Irqeita / Eminium

Irqeita (Arabic: إرقيطة or رقيطة), also spelled rgeita, commonly known as eminium[44], is a flowering plant that resembles loof in appearance. It is native to the Eastern Mediterranean. This plant is toxic if eaten raw, but the leaves can be eaten when dried or cooked thoroughly, as described in the previous section.

*irqeita stem*

Besides irqeita, the eminium plant has

---

[44] Scientific name is Eminium spiculatum.

*irqeita leaves*

several other Arabic names including danidleh (Arabic: دنيدلة), sami'aa (Arabic: سميعة or صميعة) and ja'deh al-loof (Arabic: جعدة اللوف), which is a confusing name as it also refers to other species. See ja'deh section below.

*irqeita plant*

As with other green leafy vegetables, irqeita can be frozen, either after blanching or directly from fresh after going through a pre-freezing process first. Frozen irqeita leaves are not available commercially. It can also be stored dried.

In the Southern Levant, irqeita leaves are not common at mainstream grocery stores or supermarkets. They can be sometimes bought fresh from some local grocery stores or roadside vendors if in season, or from farmers outlets. They are wild.

In the US and the UK, fresh irqeita leaves are not available in mainstream grocery stores or supermarkets, they also cannot be found in ethnic or specialised shops.

In the Southern Levant it has some culinary uses, substituting loof, which include:

1. All the culinary uses listed in the previous section.
2. In soups.
3. Stewed with meat and tahini (in

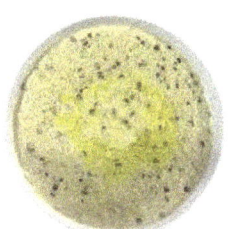

*rashouf*

Iraq).

# Ja'deh / Germander

Ja'deh (Arabic: جعدة), commonly known as germander,[45] is a shrub native to the Mediterranean which is often used for medicinal purposes.

*ja'deh plant*

The name ja'deh is often used in Arabic, locally, to name or mis-name other plants, such as loof and irqeita (both discussed earlier).

Ja'deh/germander has many localised names. These include hashishat ar-reeh (Arabic: حشيشة الريح), ju'edah (Arabic: جعيدة) and qadha (Arabic: قدحة).

Ja'deh can be stored dried.

In the Southern Levant fresh ja'deh leaves are not common at mainstream grocery stores or supermarkets. They can be sometimes bought fresh from some local grocery stores, or roadside vendors if in season, or from farmers outlets. They are wild plants. However dried leaves can be bought from markets and spice merchants.

In the US and the UK, ja'deh leaves are not available in the fresh form at mainstream grocery stores and

---

[45] Scientific name is Teucrium polium L.

supermarkets, and cannot be found in ethnic or specialised shops. Dried leaves can be bought online.

In the Southern Levant it has wide medicinal uses, but limited culinary uses where it may be substituted for loof or irqita such as:

1. In the infamous dish cha'acheel (describer earlier).

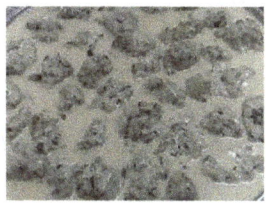

*cha'acheel*

Note however that in many articles or online postings, when recipes use the word 'ja'deh' they are, in fact, referring to loof or irqeita, as many call those two plants ja;deh in different localised dialects.

# Hweerneh / Hedge Mustard

Hweerneh or huwweira (Arabic: حويرنة or حويرة), is a leafy vegetable, often gathered wild in the Southern Levant. It has two types, one commonly known as hedge mustard with yellow flowers,[46] and one commonly known as white rocket or white wallrocket, with white flowers.[47] The leaves of these plants are eaten and the seeds are edible too. The plant is popular and has been labelled

*hweirneh plant*

*hweirneh plant*

---

[46] Scientific name is Sisymbrium officinale.
[47] Scientific name is Diplotaxis erucoides.

as 'Jericho's green gold'.[48]

*hweirneh leaves*

Besides hweirneh, the plant has other Arabic names. These include kibsa (Arabic: كبسة) and shilwah (Arabic: شِلْوَه أو شليوه).

*hweirneh sald jars*

In the Southern Levant hweirneh leaves are not usually available at mainstream grocery shops or supermarkets, but can be obtained from local markets in season. They can be obtained in season from roadside vendors who collect them.

In the US and the UK, the leaves are not readily available commercially. They may be found at some farmers markets.

As with other green leafy vegetables, hweirneh leaves can be stored frozen either after blanching, or directly from fresh by going through a pre-freezing process first. Frozen hweirneh leaves are not available commercially.

In the Levant hweirneh is used in several recipes:

1. Chopped and mixed with yogurt and olive oil, fermented for several days, then eaten with flat bread. Note that, if not available and one is craving this popular

*hweirneh with yogurt*

---

[48] https://www.alwatanvoice.com/arabic/news/2017/03/25/ 1032051.html

dish, the plant can be substituted with khardal leaves, watercress, arugula/rocket or purslane.
2. As a fresh salad chopped with lemon juice, olive oil, salt, diced onion and tomatoes.
3. With jameed, similar to the recipe with yogurt above.
4. A recipe of hweirneh and yogurt is available ready-made in jars across the Palestinian Territories and in Jordan.

# Khardal / Mustard Leaves

Khardal (Arabic: خردل) is the Arabic word for mustard. Numerous heritage culinary texts refer to 'khardal leaves' as an edible leaf vegetable when the plant is at the juvenile stage. However, there is great confusion and contradiction when references describe these leafy vegetables or try to pinpoint a specific plant. The Arabic nomenclature used to describe this plant is extremely confusing as different references refer to numerous related plants, mostly from the genus Sinapis,[49]. These plants are commonly known in English as Charlock mustard, field mustard, wild mustard, white mustard or yellow mustard. They are also grouped with the genus Brassica,[50] where the plants

*khardal plant (sinapis)*

*khardal plant (brassica)*

---

[49] Scientific names are Sinapis arvensis and Sinapis alba
[50] Scientific name is brassica nigra.

are commonly known as black mustard. The seeds for these plants are commonly used as spices.

These leafy vegetables are related, but not similar to, the more common mustard greens often found in US and UK supermarkets. They are, in fact, another species of the genus Brassica[51] and are commonly known as brown mustard, Chinese mustard, Indian mustard, leaf mustard, oriental mustard and vegetable mustard.

Some of the many names used in Arabic include khardal barri (Arabic: خردل بري, translated to wild mustard), khardala (Arabic: خردلة), lfeiteh (Arabic: لفيتة), fjeileh (Arabic: فجيلة), sefira (Arabic: ضفيرة), sfeirieh (Arabic: سفيرية), and maqra or mugara (Arabic: مقرة). Note however that these names are also sometimes used for other, different, plants in parts of the Levant and other Arab countries, which adds further complexity to the already confusing nomenclature.

In the Southern Levant, the leafy vegetable khardal leaves are not usually available in mainstream grocery shops or supermarkets. They can be obtained in season from roadside vendors who collect them.

In the US and the UK, khardal leaves

---

[51] Scientific name is brassica juncea.

are not readily available commercially, unlike their cousins, mustard greens, which are often available at mainstream supermarkets or grocery stores. They may be found at some farmers markets.

*mustard greens*

Like many other green leafy vegetables, khardal leaves can be stored frozen either after blanching, or directly from fresh by going through a pre-freezing process first. Frozen khardal leaves are not available commercially.

In the Levant, these leaves have similar culinary uses to hweirneh, indeed some people substitute these leaves for hweirneh in their recipes:

1. Sautéed with oil and diced onion, and, in some regions, egg, minced or diced meat can be added.
2. As a fresh salad with lemon juice, olive oil, salt and sumac.
3. Chopped and mixed with yogurt then eaten with flat bread.

*khardalah with yogurt*

## 'Owainah / Silene

'Owainah (Arabic: عوينة) is a flowering plant, native to the Eastern Mediterranean. In English, its common name is Palestinian/Egyptian campion

*'owainah plant*

or Egyptian catchfly.[52] The leaves of the plant are edible.

In the Southern Levant it also has several names including silinah (Arabic: سيلينة) and samamikha (Arabic: سماميخا), ein al-bint (Arabic: عين البنت), hilowlow (Arabic: حلولو), and rkika (Arabic: رقيقة or ارکیکة).

*'owainah leaves*

Several varieties of the plant are eaten around the Mediterranean, where young leaves can be eaten raw, while mature leaves can be boiled, fried, stewed or mixed into dishes. However, in Southern Europe, the plant eaten is a related species from the Silene genus, commonly known as the bladder campion or maidenstears.[53] It is a common leafy vegetable in Spain, Italy, Greece and Cyprus, where it is used in salads, risotto, stewed with chickpeas or sautéed with eggs.

*chickpea and silene stew*

In the Southern Levant, 'owainah leaves are not available at mainstream grocery shops or supermarkets. In season, they can be obtained from street and roadside vendors who gather them.

In the US and the UK, the leaves are not readily available commercially. They may be found at some farmers markets. Note that the plant is increasingly being cultivated in Southern Europe and is

---

[52] Scientific names are Silene palaestina and Silene aegyptiaca.
[53] Scientific name is Silene vulgaris.

often sold in markets.

As with other green leafy vegetables, 'owainah coarsely chopped leaves can be stored frozen either after blanching, or directly from fresh by going through a pre-freezing process first. Frozen 'owainah leaves are not available commercially.

In the Southern Levant, 'owainah leaves have culinary uses:

1. Chopped leaves are sautéed with diced onion in olive oil, mixed, instead of oregano, in a dough to make aqras, then baked in the oven.
2. As the main filling with onion and sumac in fatayer (pastry parcels), similar to the famous spinach fatayer.

*aqras 'owainah*

# Dhabh / Salsify

Dhabh[54] (Arabic: ذبح) is a flowering plant with a tubular root which belongs to the Scorzonera genus, known as salsify in English. There are numerous species native to the Mediterranean, several of these are edible, where the leaves, roots, sprouts and flowers can all be eaten.

*dhabh plant*

---

[54] Scientific name is Scorzonera papposa.

The plant has many Arabic local names including dabah (Arabic: دبح) and rubahla (Arabic: ربحلا or ربحلة) to name but two.

*dhabh plant*

The plant is related to black salsify or Spanish salsify[55]. It is widely cultivated and used as a food ingredient in Europe, where the roots, leafy shoots and open flowers are consumed both cooked and raw.

*dhabh leaves*

In the Southern Levant, dhabh leaves are not available at mainstream grocery shops or supermarkets. In season, they can be obtained from street and roadside vendors who collect them.

In the US and the UK, the leaves are not readily available commercially. A related species, black or Spanish salsify can be bought from farmer markets.

*Spanish salsify*

As with other green leafy vegetables, dhabh coarsely chopped leaves can be stored frozen either after blanching, or directly from fresh by going through a pre-freezing process first. Frozen dhabh leaves are not available commercially. The leaves can also be dried and ground down and used as a flavouring.]

In the Southern Levant the plants roots, sprouts and leaves have culinary uses, and can be used like khubeiza in many

---

[55] Scientific name is Scorzonera hispanica.

recipes:

1. Sautéed (chopped or whole) with onion in olive oil and onion.
2. Simmering or boiling the leaves to be eaten as side dish.
3. The young leaves (and flowers) are used in salads (substituting spinach, lettuce or khubeiza) mixed with salt, lemon juice and olive oil.
4. Added to bulgur in a pilaf.
5. The roots are peeled and eaten raw as a snack.

A related plant in the Southern Levant, which resembles dhabh is qa'far (Arabic: قعفر) or qa'feer (Arabic: قعفير), also known as Jordanian viper's grass.[56] Its roots can be peeled and eaten raw as a snack.

*qa'far plant*

# Kalakh / Giant Fennel

Kalakh (Arabic: كلخ), known as giant fennel[57] or common ferula, is a flowering plant native to the Mediterranean and East Africa. Unlike its distant relative common fennel,[58] whose leaves, stems, stalks, seeds and bulb are edible, kalakh is considered toxic by many, who advise us not to eat it and that its use is purely ornamental.

*kalakh plant*

---

[56] Scientific name is Scorzonera judaica.
[57] Scientific name is Ferula communis L.
[58] Scientific name is Foeniculum vulgare Mill.

Despite its abundance in the wilderness, because it is poisonous to many animals, the plant is not very popular in the Southern Levant. Despite this, it enjoys popularity in communities of the Eastern Mediterranean and North Africa who do eat this plant. The young stems and inflorescences gathered, cooked and cooled for several hours to remove the toxic effects.

Since ancient times, the resin of the Ferula species has been extracted and used for medicinal purposes. The resin of giant fennel is known as 'gum ammoniac of Morocco'.

*gum ammoniac of Morocco*

Resins of other related Ferula species are also well known and some are used as spices. One of the most famous is asafoetida,[59] commonly called the devil's dung, which is famed for its pungent smell. It is used in Persian and Indian cuisines.

In Arabic, the plant is known by other names such as boubana (Arabic: بوبنة), boubal (Arabic: بوبال) and anjadan (Arabic: أنجدان).

In the Southern Levant, kalakh is not available in mainstream grocery stores or supermarkets. The plant grows in the wild and can be gathered, in season, or purchased from roadside vendors.

---

[59] From the plant Ferula assa-foetida L.

In the US and the UK, the plant is not readily available commercially in either mainstream supermarkets or grocery stores. Dried leaves or seeds can be obtained from speciality health stores or online.

The inflorescents have a short shelf life and can be preserved in a cold place only for few days.

In parts of the Southern Levant, two of the ways that the plant is eaten are:

1. The young stems and inflorescences are boiled and the fluid is squeezed out, or it is steamed, then sautéed with diced onion in olive oil or ghee and served with yoghurt and flat bread.
2. Sautéed as above with eggs, or minced meat.

*sautéed kalakh*

In the Eastern Mediterranean, an edible mushroom, the king trumpet mushroom,[60] often grows on the plants root. These delicious mushrooms can be sautéed, braised, boiled and grilled.

Another related plant, known as zallou'[61] (Arabic: زلّوع), is famed in the Levant, where the root is used as a

*king trumpet*

*zallou' plant*

---

[60] Scientific name is Pleurotus eryngii.
[61] Scientific name is Ferula hermonis Boiss.

traditional aphrodisiac. This is known as natural or Lebanese Viagra. It is widely available at spice merchants and has recently become available as tea bags in some supermarkets and grocery stores.

*zallou' root*

*zallou' root tea bags*

# Kharfeesh / Milk Thistle

Kharfeesh (Arabic: خرفيش), is a thorny flowering plant native to the Mediterranean region. It is commonly known as milk thistle or Saint Mary's thistle.[62] The plant is versatile, with young leaves, stems, flower buds, seeds and roots all being edible.

*kharfeesh plant*

*kharfeesh stalks*

Most people consider it as the poor cousin of 'akkob – the 'star' of the thorny vegetables.

In Arabic, the plant has several local names besides kharfeesh, including salbeen (Arabic: سلبين), harshaf barri (Arabic: الحرشف البري) and shawket Mariam (Arabic: شوكة مريم).

In the Southern Levant, kharfeesh is not

---

[62] Scientific names are Silybum eburneum and Silybum marianum.

available at mainstream grocery shops or supermarkets. They grow wild and can be obtained in season from roadside vendors who collect them.

In the US and the UK, the plant is not readily available commercially at mainstream supermarkets or grocery stores. Dried leaves or seeds can be obtained from speciality health stores or online.

The stalks or stems, can be preserved in brine or as with 'akkoub, they can be blanched and frozen.

In parts of the Southern Levant, the plant is eaten as:

1. A snack or added to salads, where the stems or roots are peeled and eaten fresh.
2. The peeled stems and young leaves are sautéed with diced onion in olive oil and served with flat bread.

*sautéed kharfeesh*

The plant is related to cardoon,[63] which is widely used as food ingredient in Spain, Portugal, France and Italy. The flower buds, stems, stalks, young leaves and roots are popular in Louisiana, USA. They can be eaten raw but are also sautéed, stewed, braised, boiled, fried and can be used to flavour cheese or

*cardoon*

---

[63] Scientific name is Scorzonera hispanica.

liquor.

# Sunnariyah / Golden Thistle

Sunnariyah (Arabic: سنارية), is a thorny flowering plant native to the Mediterranean region. It is popularly known as common golden thistle or Spanish oyster thistle.⁶⁴ It is usually the plants stems that are eaten.

*sunnariyah plant*

In Arabic, the plant has several local names, besides sunnariyah, including karneinah (Arabic: كرنينة), shauk ssfar (Arabic: شوك أصفر, literally translated as yellow thorns and shauk al-asafeer (Arabic: شوك العصافير , literally translated as birds' thorns).

*sunnariyah stems*

In the Southern Levant, sunnariyah is not available at mainstream grocery shops or supermarkets. They grow wild and can be obtained in season from roadside vendors who collect them.

In the US and the UK, if they can be found, they are marketed as wild thistles or tagarninas, preserved in jars or in the form of pates or sauces online. The stalks or stems can be preserved in brine.

*tagarninas, jars*

In parts of the Southern Levant, the plant is eaten as:

---
⁶⁴ Scientific name is Scolymus hispanicus.

1. The stems are peeled and eaten fresh as a snack or added to salads.
2. The peeled stems are sautéed with olive oil and diced onion.

Note that the vegetable is popular in Spain, where it is called tagarnina and is used in stews, soups, salads, with scrambled eggs or as a pate. Also, it is eaten in Morocco in chicken or lamb stews, and in Southern Italy for a special Easter pie.

# Qurs 'Anna / Eryngo

Qurs 'anna (Arabic: قرص عنة), also spelled qurs'anna (Arabic: قرصعنة), known as field eryngo,[65] is a flowery plant native to the Eastern Mediterranean. The young leaves are edible.

The plant has several Arabic names including shindab Crete (Arabic: شنداب كريت), shuwaiket Ibrahim (Arabic: شويكة ابراهيم) and shawk al-'arqabani (Arabic: شوك العرقباني).

*qurs 'ana plant*

In the Southern Levant, Qurs 'anna leaves are not available at mainstream grocery shops or supermarkets. In season, they can be obtained in season from street and roadside vendors who

---

[65] Scientific name is Eryngium creticum.

collect them from the wild.

In the US and the UK, the leaves are not readily available commercially. They may be found at some farmers markets.

As with other green leafy vegetables, qurs 'anna coarsely chopped leaves can be stored frozen either after blanching, or directly from fresh by going through a pre-freezing process first. Frozen qurs 'anna leaves are not available commercially.

In the Southern Levant, qurs 'anna leaves have four main culinary uses:

1. Raw – coarsely chopped in salad with diced onion, lemon juice or pomegranate molasses, olive oil and salt. Tomatoes can also be added.
2. Finely chopped, as a substitute for parsley in tabbouleh salad.
3. As the main filling with onion and sumac in fatayer (pastry parcels), as with the famous spinach fatayer.
4. Pickled in brine.

*qurs 'ana salad*

## Murrar / Knapweed

Murrar[66] (Arabic: مرار), commonly

---

[66] Scientific name is Centaurea pallescens.

known as knapweed or cornflower, is a flowering thorny plant, native to the Eastern Mediterranean and Egypt. The leaves and stems of the plant are edible.

This plant is often referred to as Murrer (Arabic: مرير) and by other Arabic names, including qantarion qhahib (Arabic: قنطريون شاحب) and harrar (Arabic: هرار).

*murrar plant*

In the Southern Levant, murrar is not available at mainstream grocery shops or supermarkets. They grow wild and can be obtained in season from roadside vendors who collect them.

In the US and the UK, the plant is not available commercially at mainstream supermarkets or grocery stores. They may be found at some farmers markets.

The stalks or stems can be preserved in brine.

In the Southern Levant the plant's leaves have four main culinary uses:

1. Sautéed with oil and diced onion.
2. As a salad where the leaves are chopped, boiled and pressed then mixed with diced onion, lemon juice and olive oil.
3. As a salad with yogurt called mu'assarah.
4. Raw – peeled and eaten as a snack.

# Qataf / Saltbush

Qataf (Arabic: قطف), known as Mediterranean saltbush,[67] sea orache, shrubby orache, silvery orache and tree/sea purslane, is a common bushy plant that has been harvested by humans as a food ingredient for centuries It is disappearing from our awareness having been replaced with the popular spinach leaves. Qataf leaves are edible raw and are tasty in salads. They can also be boiled or steamed and eaten like spinach. Saltbush plants are also used as ornamental plants in landscaping and can be used to prevent soil erosion in coastal areas. The plants can be found at some garden centres. A related species, garden orache (known as red orache or French orache)[68] can be bought from farmer markets. For medicinal uses they can be obtained from spice merchants.

*qataf leaves*

*red orache*

The plant has many Arabic names including rughl (Arabic: رغل), sarma (Arabic: سرمة), sarmag (Arabic: سرمق) and baql dhahabi (Arabic: بقل ذهبي).

In Australia, the dried ground leaves and seeds are used by indigenous people to flavour foods. The leaves are also sometimes eaten fresh or added to

---

[67] Scientific name is Atriplex halimus.
[68] Scientific name is Atriplex hortensis. Atriplex halimus

meat as it cooked. Recently the plant is gaining popularity as a food ingredient and is used in fresh salads and stir fries.

In the Southern Levant, qataf leaves are not available in mainstream grocery stores or supermarkets. They can be obtained in season from street and roadside vendors who collect them.

In the US and the UK, the leaves are not readily available commercially.

As with other green leafy vegetables, qataf coarsely chopped leaves can be stored frozen either after blanching, or directly from fresh by going through a pre-freezing process first. Frozen qataf leaves are not available commercially. The leaves can also be dried and ground down and used as a flavouring.

*dried qataf whole leaves*

*dried qataf leaves*

In the Southern Levant the plant's leaves have the following culinary uses:

1. Boiled, the water pressed out, then sautéed with oil and diced onion. No salt is required.
2. As a salad where the leaves are chopped, boiled and water squeezed out, then mixed with diced onion, lemon juice and olive oil. No salt is required.

*qataf salad*

# Qizha / Nigella Seeds Paste

Qizha (Arabic: قزحة) is a black coloured paste made from roasted crushed Nigella seeds. Nigella seeds, also known as black caraway or kalonji, are the seeds of the plant Nigella.[69] Many erroneously refer to it as black cumin, which is in fact the seed of another plant.[70]

*Nigella plant*

In Arabic, Nigella seeds are known as habbat al-barakeh (Arabic: حبة البركة) shouneez (Arabic: شونيز) or al-habba al-sawdaa' (Arabic: الحبة السوداء, meaning the black seed).

*Nigella seeds*

The taste of qizha is sharp and bitter with hints of sweetness. It is an acquired taste. Opinions about its taste could be compared to the British savoury spread 'Marmite', you either love it or hate it! Moreover, its appearance is rather unappetising. In a special program discussing if the world was ready for this Palestinian dish, the BBC described its appearance as being similar to engine oil![71]

*qizha paste*

Nigella seeds are common and easily available worldwide. They can be used as a stand-alone ingredient or as part of spice-mix in all kinds of recipes. In the

*Nabulsi cheese with Nigella seeds*

---

[69] Scientific name is Nigella sativa.
[70] Scientific name is Elwendia persica.
[71] https://www.bbc.com/travel/article/20190327-is-the-world-ready-for-this-palestinian-dish

Southern Levant, besides being the main ingredient in qizha, the seeds are used in the making of many breads and pastries or as a seasoning in cheeses (see Nabulsi Cheese above).

Qizha, in the form of paste in a jar, is available at some mainstream groceries and supermarkets in the Southern Levant.

*qizha jar*

In the UK and the US, qizha, sometimes marketed as black seed honey, is seldom available at mainstream outlets. It can be found at some ethnic grocery shops, or online.

In the Southern Levant qizha can be used:

1. As a spread mixed with other condiments, such as tahini, honey or dibis (date syrup)
2. Used as the defining ingredient, baked into a semolina pie.
3. As a base to a variation of traditional tahini halwa.

*qizha pie*

# 'Ijer / Young Watermelon

Watermelon[72] (Arabic: بطيخ, pronounced battikh) is one the most cultivated fruits in the world. When

*watermelon plant and fruit*

---

[72] Scientific name is Citrullus lanatus.

ripe, watermelon is a sweet, popularly eaten fruit. The flesh and the seeds are edible. Not many people know that the rind is also edible, although it is often discarded.

'Ijer (Arabic: عجر) is the name of young unripe watermelon fruits. It is well known in the Gaza Strip and Northern Sinai, where it is considered a popular vegetable when in season. Note that, unlike other fruits, watermelons stop ripening after they have been harvested.

While watermelon is available at grocery stores, supermarkets and local markets worldwide, the availability of 'ijer differs, as young, unripe watermelons will often be discarded.

In the Southern Levant, 'ijer is not available at mainstream grocery stores or supermarkets, but can be bought from local markets and street vendors in the Gaza Strip and Northern Sinai. In other parts of the region, one has to get it directly from farms.

*'ijer in market*

In the US and the UK, Ijer is not available in mainstream outlets. It may be obtained from farmers markets or directly from farms.

In the Southern Levant 'ijer is very popular in the one area as indicated above, but it is unknown by most people elsewhere. In Northern Sinai a dish made from 'ijer is called lsaimah - is considered the national dish. The culinary uses of the vegetable are:

1. Roasted on a fire, then the flesh is removed or cooked with freshly baked bread – fatteh, lsaimeh.
2. Stewed, with or without meat, where it is cooked similarly to courgettes or okra.
3. Pickled.

*fattet 'ijer*

# Habb Qraish / Aleppo Pine Seeds

Habb Qraish (Arabic: حب قريش), as it is colloquially known in the Southern Levant, is the seed of the Aleppo pine,[73] a variety of a pine tree native to the Mediterranean region. Habb Qraish seeds are considered the poor relative of the highly valued and more popular pine nuts which are replacing them in many places. Still, they are an important ingredient in many Southern Levantine dishes and sweets.

*Aleppo pines leaves and cones*

In the Southern Levant, habb Qraish is often bought from grocery stores and supermarkets and spice merchants.

In the US and the UK, habb Qraish can be found at specialised organic stores or health shops. It can be bought online. In

*habb Qraish*

---

[73] Scientific name is Pinus halepensis.

addition, the Aleppo pine seed paste, zgougou, is available in some European countries.

Despite their ready availability in the Southern Levant, the seeds of habb Qraish, also known as snobber Halabi (Arabic: صنوبر حلبي) are not widely used as a main ingredient in the cuisine. They are often used as a minor ingredient in several ways:

*zgougou paste*

1. As an ingredient in variations of duqqa (see above) called qalia (Arabic: قليّة).
2. Added to traditional sweets like malban, fruit leather (made of semolina and grape juice) and khabisa, which is a variation of the former.
3. As a snack, raw or roasted.
4. In a type of halawa.
5. Additional seasoning to flavour some cheeses.
6. A dessert called madqoqa, where raisins, habb Qraish (and sometimes dried fig and butum) plus crushed walnut, are ground in a mortar and pestle or together in a food processor, then formed into balls. Then it is covered sesame seed and flour.

*malban*

Outside the Levant, habb Qraish is the main ingredient of a traditional Tunisian pudding called 'assidet zgougou and a related Maltese dessert.

# Ballout / Acorn

Ballout (Arabic: بلوط) is the name given in Arabic to the nut of the ballout or sindian (Arabic: سنديان) tree. In English, the nut of the Oak tree is called an acorn.[74]

*ballout leaves and fruit*

Although ballout is a commonly found tree around the Mediterranean, most people are not aware that its fruit and nuts are edible. Historically, the nuts were used for food only in drought seasons or during famine conditions, but the sustainable living trend is encouraging some to reconsider the position of the acorn.

Currently there are limited culinary uses of the ballout nut worldwide. The most notable one is the processing of the nuts into flour, which can then be mixed with other flour types.

In the Southern Levant, ballout is not available in mainstream grocery stores or supermarkets. It can be obtained from farms or spice merchants.

In the US and the UK, ballout can be found at specialised organic stores or health shops mostly as flour, but rarely as a whole nut, however both forms of the nut can be bought online.

---

[74] Scientific name is Quercus.

As a culinary ingredient, ballout nuts can be used as follows:

1. Roasted and eaten as a snack.
2. Turned into flour and used to bake breads, cakes, etc.

In Algeria, ballout-based couscous is popular in some parts and there has been a revival in usage, as evident by many internet posts recently.

*acorn flour*

## Butum / Terebinth

Butum (Arabic: بطم), known as the terebinth or turpentine tree,[75] is a native of the Mediterranean, related to the pistachio tree. It is long-living tree, with some believed to be over one thousand years old.[76] The Arabic names include the closely related Mount Atlas mastic tree, Cyprus turpentine tree or Persian turpentine tree.[77] For gastronomic purposes, the tree's fruits and resins are used, as are as its young leaves.

In the Southern Levant, butum can be bought from some grocery stores and supermarkets and spice merchants, mostly dry, sometimes fresh in season.

*butum fruit*

---

[75] Scientific names Pistacia terebinthus L., a synonym Pistacia palaestina
[76] https://www.encyclopedia.com/plants-and-animals/plants/plants/terebinth
[77] Scientific name is Pistacia atlantica.

In the US and the UK, fresh butum fruits are not available at mainstream grocery stores and supermarkets. Dried fruits can be bought from specialised shops and online.

Butum has several culinary uses in the Southern Levant as:

1. Raw, as a fruit.
2. As an ingredient in variations of duqqa or zaatar (see above), where it is roasted and ground, then mixed with other ingredients (Arabic: قَلْيَة).
3. Ground down into flour and baked as bread.
4. Mixed with dried fruits into wheat bread.
5. A dessert called madqoqa, where raisins, habb Qraish, dried figs and butum, are mixed in a mortar and pestle or food processed together, then formed into balls. Then it is covered with sesame seed and flour.
6. As a kibbeh.
7. Used as a flavouring in kishk.
8. In spring, the young shoots are chopped up, mixed into salads with garlic, ground chilli and husrum.
9. The resin is used similarly to mastic (the resin of the mastic tree traditionally produced on

*dried butum*

*fresh butum fruit*

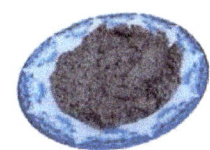

*butum bread*

*butum kibbeh*

*terebinth resin*

the island Chios, Greece, which is used as flavouring or gum)[78] as a chewing gum.

# Sidr / Christ's Thorn Jujube

Sidr (Arabic: سدر), known as Christ's thorn jujube[79] is an ancient tree, native to Western Asia and Africa. It produces edible sweet fruits, eaten in the Levant since ancient times.

*sidr tree and fruit*

The fruit has other Arabic names including zufayzef (Arabic: زفيزف) and nabeq (Arabic: نبق). The nomenclature is confusing as the same name refers to another distant relative genus, namely buckthorns, which has numerous species.[80] It also refers to the tree species sea buckthorn[81] (Arabic: نبق البحر, pronounced nabeq al-bahr), which also bears similar looking fruits and is popular in Europe. Another confusing name is dawm (Arabic: دوم), which often refers to the fruits of the tree chamaerops,[82] which is not edible.

*chamaerops*

*sea buckthorn*

Moreover, the sidr tree is not to be confused with two other related trees that bear similar fruits. The first is the

*Jerusalem thorn*

---

[78] Scientific name is Pistacia lentiscus.
[79] Scientific name is Ziziphus spina-christi.
[80] Scientific name is Rhamnus.
[81] Scientific name is Hippophae rhamnoides.
[82] Scientific name is Chamaerops humilis.

jujube[83] tree (Arabic: عناب, pronounced 'innab), whose fruits are also eaten worldwide and are popular in the Southern Levant. The second is the Jerusalem thorn[84] (Arabic: شبهان شوك المسيح, pronounced shibhan shawk al-maseeh – translated paliurus of Christ's thorn). This is not to be confused with another plant, also called commonly the Jerusalem thorn[85] from the Parkinsonia genus.

*Jerusalem thorn (parkinsonia)*

In the Southern Levant, the fresh fruit is available at grocery stores and supermarkets when in season, and can be bought from local markets. Sidr jam is also available.

In the US and the UK, the fresh fruit is seldom available in mainstream grocery stores or supermarkets and is rarely available at ethnic grocery stores. The jam can be obtained online. Also, sidr powder can be obtained online as soap substitute.

*sidr jam*

Sidr fruits have three main culinary uses in the Southern Levant:

1. Eaten raw as fruits.
2. Made into jams.
3. Dried and ground into flour used in breads and sweet pastries.

*sidr fruit*

A famous honey is sidr honey, which is

*sidr powder*

---
[83] Scientific name is Ziziphus jujuba.
[84] Scientific name is Paliurus spina-christi.
[85] Scientific name is Parkinsonia aculeata L..

a mono-floral honey made solely from the nectar of sidr trees in Yemen. The honey is expensive due to its wide medical uses in the Middle East.

*sidr honey*

From cultural point of view, the sidr tree is important. In Islamic tradition, it is considered to be Sidrat al-Muntaha, the lote tree mentioned in the Quran. In Christianity, the spiny branches of the tree are known as one of two trees (the other is Jerusalem thorn) used to make the crown of thorns put on the head of Jesus Christ before crucifixion.

# Part III
# Definitions

In this final part of the book, I explain some of the nomenclature used to describe the dishes or recipes mentioned in Parts 1 and 2.

This not a comprehensive glossary, but rather it lists the most important names, many of which appeared repeatedly in the preceding pages.

## *Aqras*
Sometimes used as an interchangeable word to fatayer (see below), but in many instances, it is used to describe a type of small backed, flat bread, made of dough mixed with ingredients such as wild oregano and olive oil.

## *Baba Ghanouj*
A Levantine dip made of mashed cooked aubergine/eggplant, olive oil, lemon juice, various seasonings and sometimes tahini.

## *Bahboutha*
Balls of dough cooked in broth and added to leafy vegetables such as khubeiza or loof.

## *Cha'acheel*
Dumplings made of flour, eggs, onion and a leafy vegetable, such as loof, cooked in boiled jameed (and lentils).

### Dibis
Also pronounced as dibs, which means molasses. It usually describes any syrup, but especially from a fruit extract or spice infusion, with the word 'dibis' preceding the ingredient, such as sumac dibis or pomegranate dibis.

### Falafel
Deep-fried balls or patties made of made of a mixture of chickpeas (or fava beans), fresh herbs and spices.

### Fatayer
Pastry parcels or pies stuffed with spinach, cheese or many other variations and baked. Alternatively, the pastry can be in the form of open pie, topped with minced meat or cheese.

### Fatteh
Pieces of cut flatbread - fresh, toasted, grilled, or stale, covered with other ingredients such as hummus, yogurt or added to broth.

### Fattoush
A Levantine salad made of chopped tomatoes, cucumber, bell peppers, radish, sumac and cut (sometimes fried or toasted) bread.

### Ijjeh
Also spelled ejjeh, this is a small omelette or savoury egg pancake, typically filled with a fresh mixture of

herbs and diced vegetables such as courgette/zucchini.

## *Hummus*

Literally chickpea, is a Levantine dip, made from cooked, mashed chickpeas, blended with tahini, lemon juice, and garlic. The standard hummus garnish includes olive oil, a few whole chickpeas, parsley, paprika and sometimes fried minced meat with pine nuts. Many variations exist with different ingredients mixed into the mixture such as roasted pepper.

## *Kebab*

Minced meat, often mutton or lamb, but regional recipes may include beef, goat, chicken, fish and rarely pork. Flavoured with spices and herbs, sometimes with vegetables. Typically cooked on a skewer, over a fire or it can be baked in a pan, oven or prepared as a stew.

## *Kibbeh or kubbeh*

Also spelled kubba, it is made by pounding bulgur, together with meat, (often mutton or lamb, but also beef, goat, chicken, fish and rarely pork), into a fine paste that can be shaped into hollow balls filled with minced meat, onion, with toasted pine nuts and spices then deep fried, grilled or boiled. It may also be layered and cooked/baked on a tray or served raw. Some variations substitute bulgur with rice or jareesh.

## *Kufta*
Consist of minced meat, usually lamb or mutton, beef, chicken, (rarely pork) or a mixture of them, then mixed with spices, herbs and sometimes other ingredients. It is shaped into meatballs, patties or spread flat on trays to be baked

## *Kullaj*
Similar to baklava, this is a special kind of dough, stuffed with Nabulsi cheese, walnut or pistachio, baked in the oven then covered with sweet syrup, as desired.

## *Kunafa*
A traditional Levantine dessert made with shredded filo pastry dough, over a layer of sweetened Nabulsi or Akkawi cheese, topped with sugar syrup then garnished with pistachio and pine nuts.

## *Mahshi/Mahashi*
Stuffed vegetables or wrapped green leaves filled with rice, bulgur or freekeh, with herbs, spices and, in many instances, minced meat. Examples include courgette/zucchini, aubergine /eggplant, vine leaves and cabbage leaves.

## *Mansaf*
Jordan's national dish, made of lamb, cooked in a sauce of jameed

and spices, then served with rice (regional varieties can use jareesh or bulgur). Other varieties use chicken instead of lamb.

## Manaeesh

Also spelled manaqish, manakeesh, manaeesh. This plural term for manqousha, is a baked dough, topped with savoury ingredient such as zaatar, cheese or minced meat. Similar to a pizza, it can be sliced or folded.

## Maqloubeh

Also spelled maqlouba, maqluba or maqlooba. It literally means 'upside-down'. It is a dish made of rice, meat, poultry and one or more variations of vegetables (often fried), then cooked together in a pot, which is flipped upside down when served.

## Mawaleh

An encompassing term that refers to a collection of savoury baked pastry dishes such as breadsticks, cookies, and petits fours, that are often flavoured with spices and herbs, such as zaatar.

## Mufarrakeh

Also spelled mofarrakah, it is traditionally made of potato, egg and spices, fried in oil or ghee, but unlike ijjeh, it is not intact - the egg crumbles apart around the potatoes. Other vegetables can substitute the potato, such as akkoub.

### *Mu'ajjanat*
An encompassing term for baked pastries.

### *Musakhan*
Palestine's national dish which is made of sumac, chicken, onion and olive oil over taboon flat bread. It is baked in a taboon or tannur (tandoor) clay oven.

### *Mutabbal*
A Levantine dip made with roasted aubergine/eggplants, garlic, tahini or yogurt, lemon, and salt. Garnished with olive oil, parsley and pomegranate.

### *Mutabbaq*
Literally means folded, this is a thinly spread dough, either filled with savoury or sweet ingredients such as wild oregano or cheese, baked with lots of olive oil.

### *Qatayef*
Also spelled katayef. This is a dessert commonly served during the month of Ramadan. A sort of sweet dumpling, filled with cream or nuts. It could be described as a folded pancake.

### *Rashouf*
A thick soup/porridge-like dish

made of lentils, jareesh, bulgur, jameed or sometimes chickpea, topped with fried onion and ghee (samneh).

### *Ruzz Mfalfal*
The Arabic version of pilaf rice, where the rice is sautéed slightly with oil or ghee, sometimes vermicelli is also added and then water, salt and stock, or spices are added, brought to the boil, then simmered.

### *Shawarma*
Meat, (traditionally lamb, mutton or chicken), cut into thin slices, stacked in a cone-like shape and roasted on a slowly-turning vertical rotisserie or spit. Nowadays other types of meat can be used including turkey, beef, or veal.

### *Sfeiha*
Spelled also sfiha or sfeeha, this is a flatbread shaped dough, baked with a minced meat topping, often lamb, flavoured with onion, tomato, pine nuts and spices.

### *Shish Barak / Shush Barak*
Also called adhan al-shayeb, these are ravioli-like dumplings filled with seasoned lamb and onions. They are boiled, baked or fried then served in a warm yogurt or jameed sauce with mint, coriander, other herbs and spices.

### Tahini

Also spelled tahina, this is a condiment made from toasted ground, hulled sesame seeds. It is a major ingredient in Levantine cuisine. It is most famously used in hummus, baba ghanoush and halva.

### Tabbouleh

This is a Levantine salad, traditionally made of finely chopped parsley, tomatoes, mint, onion bulgur then seasoned with olive oil, lemon juice, salt and sweet pepper. Newer variations are numerous, including using quinoa instead of bulgur, or substituting parsley for spinach.

www.ingramcontent.com/pod-product-compliance
Lightning Source LLC
Chambersburg PA
CBHW070456090426
42735CB00012B/2572